TRADE ISSUES, POLICIES AND LAWS

THE TRANS-PACIFIC PARTNERSHIP

KEY PROVISIONS AND STRATEGIC IMPLICATIONS

Trade Issues, Policies and Laws

Additional books in this series can be found on Nova's website under the Series tab.

Additional e-books in this series can be found on Nova's website under the eBooks tab.

TRADE ISSUES, POLICIES AND LAWS

THE TRANS-PACIFIC PARTNERSHIP

KEY PROVISIONS AND STRATEGIC IMPLICATIONS

DEREK PIERCE
EDITOR

nova publishers
New York

Library of Congress Cataloging-in-Publication Data

ISBN: 978-1-53610-195-9

Published by Nova Science Publishers, Inc. † New York

CONTENTS

PREFACE

The Trans-Pacific Partnership (TPP) is a proposed free trade agreement (FTA) among the United States and 11 Asia-Pacific countries. The U.S. Trade Representative (USTR) has described it as a "comprehensive and high standard" agreement, designed to eliminate and reduce trade barriers and to establish and extend the rules and disciplines of the trading system among the parties to the agreement. If implemented, it would be the largest plurilateral FTA by value of trade, encompassing roughly 40% of world GDP, and could serve further to integrate the United States in the dynamic Asia-Pacific region. As a "living agreement," it has the potential to negotiate new rules and expand its membership. It could also mark a shift to the negotiation of "mega-regional" trade liberalization agreements in lieu of bilateral FTAs and broader multilateral trade liberalization in the World Trade Organization (WTO). This book examines the key provisions of the proposed TPP, related policy and economic contexts, and issues of potential interest to Congress.

In: The Trans-Pacific Partnership
Editor: Derek Pierce
ISBN: 978-1-53610-195-9

Chapter 1

THE TRANS-PACIFIC PARTNERSHIP (TPP): KEY PROVISIONS AND ISSUES FOR CONGRESS*

Ian F. Fergusson and Brock R. Williams

SUMMARY

The Trans-Pacific Partnership (TPP) is a proposed free trade agreement (FTA) among 12 Asia- Pacific countries, with both economic and strategic significance for the United States. The proposed agreement is perhaps the most ambitious FTA undertaken by the United States in terms of its size, the breadth and depth of its commitments, its potential evolution, and its geo-political significance. Signed on February 4, 2016, after several years of negotiations, if implemented, TPP would be the largest FTA in which the United States participates, and would eliminate trade barriers and establish new trade rules and disciplines on a range of issues among TPP partners not found in previous U.S. FTAs or the World Trade Organization (WTO). In addition, the TPP is designed to better integrate the United States into the growing Asia-Pacific region and has become the economic centerpiece of the Administration's "rebalance" to the region. Congress would need to enact implementing

* This is an edited, reformatted and augmented version of a Congressional Research Service publication R44489, prepared for Members and Committees of Congress dated June 14, 2016.

legislation for the agreement to enter into force for the United States. Such legislation would be considered under Trade Promotion Authority (TPA) procedures, unless Congress determines the Administration has not met TPA requirements.

TPP Members

Currently, the TPP includes Australia, Brunei, Canada, Chile, Japan, Malaysia, Mexico, New Zealand, Peru, Singapore, the United States, and Vietnam, which together comprise 40% of the world's GDP. TPP is envisioned as a "living agreement," potentially addressing new issues and open to future members, including as a possible vehicle to advance a wider Asia-Pacific free trade area. The United States currently has FTAs with six TPP partner countries. Japan is the largest economy and trading partner without an existing U.S. FTA. Malaysia and Vietnam also stand out among TPP countries without existing U.S. FTAs, given the rapid growth in U.S. trade with the two nations over the past three decades and their generally higher level of trade restrictions.

Potential Outcomes of TPP

The TPP would provide several principal trade liberalization and rules-based outcomes for the United States. These include the following:

- lower tariff and nontariff barriers on U.S. goods through eventual elimination of all tariffs on industrial products and most tariffs and quotas on agricultural products;
- greater service sector liberalization with enhanced disciplines, such as nondiscriminatory and minimum standard of treatment, along with certain exceptions;
- additional intellectual property rights protections in patent, copyrights, trademarks, and trade secrets; first specific data protection provisions for biologic drugs and new criminal penalties for cybertheft of trade secrets;
- investment protections that guarantee nondiscriminatory treatment, minimum standard of treatment and other provisions to protect foreign

investment, balanced by provisions to protect a state's right to regulate in the public interest;

- enforceable provisions designed to provide minimum standards of labor and environmental protection in TPP countries;
- commitments, without an enforcement mechanism, to avoid currency manipulation, provide transparency and reporting concerning monetary policy, and engage in regulatory dialogue among TPP parties;
- digital trade commitments to promote the free flow of data and to prevent data localization, except for data localization in financial services, alongside commitments on privacy and exceptions for legitimate public policy purposes;
- enhanced regulatory transparency and due process provisions in standards-setting; and
- the most expansive disciplines on state-owned enterprises ever in a U.S. FTA or the WTO, albeit with exceptions, to advance fair competition with private firms based on commercial considerations.

The U.S. International Trade Commission (USITC) has estimated that the TPP would bring modest overall benefits to the U.S. economy once implemented, slightly increasing both output (0.15%) and employment (0.07%) above a baseline scenario without the agreement. According to the USITC study, most agriculture and services sectors would see expansions, while some manufacturing and natural resources sectors would be expected to contract relative to baseline projections as resources shifted within the U.S. economy.

TPP Debate

Views on the likely effects of the agreement vary. Proponents argue that the TPP is in the national interest and has the potential to boost economic growth and jobs through expanded trade and investment opportunities in what many see as the world's most economically vibrant region. Opponents of TPP voice concerns over possible job loss and competition in import-sensitive industries. Other concerns include how a TPP agreement might limit the government's ability to regulate in areas such as health, food safety, and the environment. The Obama Administration and others have argued that the strategic value of a TPP agreement parallels its economic value, while others argue that past trade pacts have had a limited impact on broad foreign policy dynamics. In analyzing the agreement and its implementing legislation, Congress may consider the agreement from several of these perspectives, as well as how the TPP promotes progress on U.S. trade negotiating objectives.

INTRODUCTION

The Trans-Pacific Partnership (TPP) is a proposed free trade agreement (FTA) among the United States and 11 Asia-Pacific countries. The U.S. Trade Representative (USTR) has described it as a "comprehensive and high standard" agreement, designed to eliminate and reduce trade barriers and to establish and extend the rules and disciplines of the trading system among the parties to the agreement (see **Figure 1**).[1] If implemented, it would be the largest plurilateral FTA by value of trade, encompassing roughly 40% of world GDP, and could serve further to integrate the United States in the dynamic Asia-Pacific region. As a "living agreement," it has the potential to negotiate new rules and expand its membership. It could also mark a shift to the negotiation of "mega-regional" trade liberalization agreements in lieu of bilateral FTAs and broader multilateral trade liberalization in the World Trade Organization (WTO).

The 12 countries concluded the TPP negotiations and released the text of the agreement in late 2015. Trade ministers from the TPP countries signed the final agreement text on February 4, 2016, and several countries are seeking to ratify the agreement this year. TPP draws congressional interest on a number of fronts, and Congress must approve implementing legislation for U.S. commitments under the agreement to enter into force. The TPP would be eligible to receive expedited legislative consideration under Trade Promotion Authority (TPA), P.L. 114-26, unless Congress determines the Administration has failed to advance TPA negotiating objectives, or has not met various notification and consultation requirements.[2] Furthermore, the TPP may affect a range of sectors and regions of the U.S. economy and could influence the shape and path of U.S. trade policy for the foreseeable future. It may also serve strategic goals of the United States by strengthening regional alliances and extending U.S. influence in the Asia-Pacific region. This report examines the key provisions of the proposed TPP, related policy and economic contexts, and issues of potential interest to Congress.

Background

The precursor to the TPP was the Trans-Pacific Strategic Economic Partnership (P-4). It was conceived in 2003 by Singapore, New Zealand, and Chile as a path to trade liberalization in the Asia-Pacific region—Brunei joined in 2005—and the P-4 agreement was concluded in 2006. U.S. trade policymakers took notice of the P-4's relative ambition as a possible template for a wider Asia-Pacific free trade agreement. President Bush notified Congress of his intention to negotiate with the existing P-4 members on September 22, 2008, along with Australia, Peru, and Vietnam, on December 30, 2008, as required under past and current TPA. President Obama recommitted to the TPP negotiations in November 2009 and renotified Congress of the Administration's intention to negotiate the renamed Trans-Pacific Partnership. In October 2010, the TPP participants agreed by consensus to the inclusion of Malaysia as a negotiating partner.

The negotiating partners announced a framework for the agreement at the sidelines of the Asia- Pacific Economic Cooperation (APEC) Ministerial in Honolulu, HI, November 8-13, 2011. Thereafter, Canada, Mexico, and Japan consulted with the existing TPP partners on joining the negotiations. The North American Free Trade Agreement (NAFTA) partners—Canada and Mexico–acceded to the negotiations in December 2012, followed by Japan in July 2013.[3] During the course of the negotiations, others countries, such as South Korea, Taiwan, and the Philippines expressed varying degrees of interest in joining, but the parties decided to conclude the agreement before contemplating new members. The agreement must be ratified by all parties to enter into force in the first two years from its 2016 signing. Thereafter, it requires at least six countries representing 85% of the bloc's 2013 gross domestic product (GDP) to accede to the agreement for it to take effect, thus requiring ratification by the United States and Japan for entry into force to occur.

Congressional Consideration

The Bipartisan Comprehensive Trade Priorities and Accountability Act of 2015 (P.L. 114-26), the current grant of TPA (TPA-2015), sets the procedures governing congressional consideration of the proposed TPP. TPA is the authority by which Congress, for specific periods of time, sets trade negotiating objectives, establishes notification and consultation requirements, and enables implementing legislation for reciprocal trade agreements to be considered under expedited procedures if it meets certain statutory requirements. TPA-2015 was enacted into law on June 29, 2015, and expires in 2018, with a possible extension to 2021.

Legislation to implement the TPP can be considered under the expedited procedures of TPA, since the TPP was signed during the time TPA has been effect. The TPP could be considered under expedited procedures during this Congress, the next Congress, or even after the present grant of TPA expires. TPP was signed and the final text of the agreement was released on February 4, 2016. Following signature, under TPA, implementing legislation can be introduced 30 days after the release of the final text of the agreement on a day when both Houses are in session. That day was March 14, 2016. The President notified Congress of the changes to U.S. law that TPP implementation would require on April 1, 2016. A TPA-required report by the U.S. International Trade Commission (USITC) on the potential economic effects of the agreement was released on May 18, 2016. Once the President submits the legislation for introduction, TPA sets a 90-legislative-day deadline for congressional consideration with set periods for committee and floor consideration by the House and Senate.[4]

TPP's Strategic Context[5]

The TPP could have significant implications beyond its direct economic impact, in what many term as broader "strategic" contexts. Obama Administration officials and other TPP proponents argue that these implications would be positive and felt in several ways, both geo-economic and geo-political. Though such implications are hard to define precisely, proponents of the TPP's strategic importance suggest that the United States could use the agreement as a tool to exert influence in the region and beyond, in not only economic, but also broader political and security spheres.

Administration officials regularly emphasize the TPP's strategic value in arguing for its approval. USTR Ambassador Froman said in a 2014 speech:

(in billions of dollars)

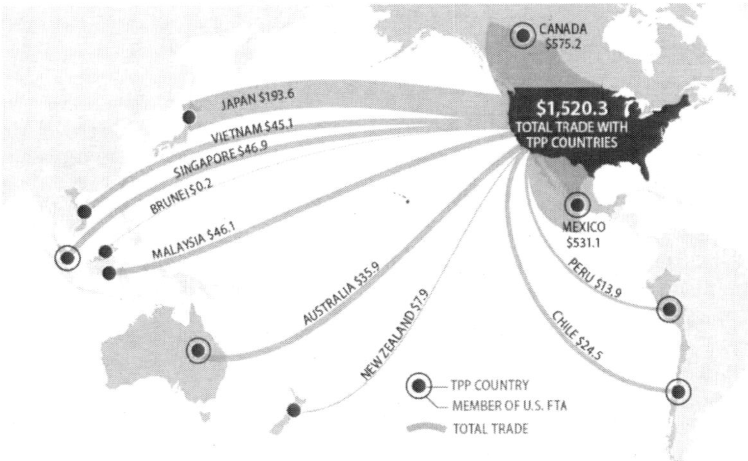

Trans-Pacific Partnership Countries

	U.S. FTA	Population (millions)	GDP ($billions)	U.S. Imports ($billions)	U.S. Exports ($billions)	Trade Balance ($billions)
Australia	✔	23.6	1,443	10.9	25.0	14.2
Brunei		0.4	17	0.0	0.1	0.1
Canada	✔	35.5	1,785	295.2	280.0	-15.2
Chile	✔	17.8	258	8.9	15.6	6.7
Japan		127.1	4,602	131.1	62.5	-68.6
Malaysia		30.6	338	33.8	12.3	-21.5
Mexico	✔	119.7	1,291	294.7	236.4	-58.4
New Zealand		4.6	198	4.3	3.6	-0.6
Peru	✔	31.4	203	5.1	8.8	3.7
Singapore	✔	5.5	308	18.2	28.7	10.4
Vietnam		90.6	186	38.0	7.1	-30.9
United States		319.1	17,348	Total U.S. Imports **$840.2**	Total U.S. Exports **$680.1**	Total U.S. Trade Balance **-$160.1**

$U.S. DOLLARS

Source: Analysis by CRS. Population and GDP data from IMF, World Economic Outlook, October 2015. Trade data from the U.S. International Trade Commission (USITC).

Notes: Trade data only includes goods trade, and are from 2015. GDP and population data are from 2014.

Figure 1. Trans-Pacific Partnership Countries.

> TPP is as important strategically as it is economically. Economically, TPP would bind together a group that represents 40 percent of global GDP and about a third of world trade. Strategically, TPP is the avenue through which the United States, working with nearly a dozen other countries (and another half dozen waiting in the wings), is playing a leading role in writing the [trade] rules of the road for a critical region in flux.[6]

Secretary of State John Kerry wrote in 2015:

> TPP also matters for reasons far beyond trade. The Asia-Pacific includes three of the globe's four most populous countries and its three largest economies. Going forward, that region is going to have a big say in shaping international rules of the road on the Internet, financial regulation, maritime security, the environment, and many other areas of direct concern to the United States. Remember that, in our era, economic and security issues overlap; we can't lead on one and lag on the other.[7]

Overall, proponents maintain that through the TPP, the United States can further a wide range of goals, including the following:

- liberalizing trade, encouraging market-oriented reforms, and driving economic growth;
- establishing and updating regional trade rules and disciplines consistent with U.S. interests and modern commercial realities;
- potentially strengthening the global trade architecture;
- strengthening regional alliances and partnerships;
- maintaining U.S. leadership and influence in the Asia-Pacific region; and
- enhancing U.S. national security.

In terms of economic influence, some observers argue the TPP may present an alternative to FTAs constructed by other countries, especially in the Asia-Pacific region. Such agreements often exclude or have less extensive provisions on agriculture, services, investment, and intellectual property rights (IPR), which some see as among the most important FTA provisions for certain U.S. sectors; moreover, these agreements generally have few if any binding protections for worker rights and the environment. The TPP could provide participating governments political cover to enact reforms relating to these and other provisions, presenting them as a tradeoff for greater access to the large U.S. market. While debate continues, both in the United States and abroad, over the appropriate scope of various TPP provisions and the degree to which they differ from other regional pacts, some policymakers argue that the TPP would provide the United States with leverage to help shape regional and, perhaps, broader multilateral economic norms.[8]

In the geo-political realm, some analysts consider the TPP to be a litmus test for U.S. credibility in the Asia-Pacific region. Proponents argue the TPP signals the primacy of U.S. integration into Asia's economic and diplomatic structures, suggesting that congressional inaction or rejection of the TPP would make the Administration's rebalancing strategy look relatively weak and the United States look divided on how important it considers its leadership role in the region.[9] Similarly, many Asian policymakers—correctly or not—could interpret a failure of the TPP in the United States as a symbol of declining U.S. interest in the region and its inability to assert leadership.[10] Some critics of the TPP assert that such arguments are overstated, and that the strength or weakness of broader bilateral political and security relationships depend more on countries' assessment of their political and security interests than on whether they have a trade agreement with the United States.[11]

China is not a TPP member, but its emergence as a regional economic power with active overseas trade and investment initiatives forms an important backdrop to the TPP's consideration. Those championing the TPP, including President Obama, often cast it as a vehicle for maintaining U.S. leadership in Asia in the face of China's rise, arguing that through the agreement, the United States can "write the rules" for regional trade and investment and help foster a broader, rules- based regional order.[12] Others contend that casting the TPP as an effort to "counter" Chinese initiatives is unproductive, and could create negative perceptions of U.S. intentions, both in China and elsewhere in the region. Some also argue that in many ways U.S. and Chinese goals for trade liberalization and rules and norms in the region could be mutually reinforcing, rather than competing, by promoting the goal of free trade in the Asia-Pacific region[13]

Trade agreements, and trade policy in general, inevitably exist at the intersection of domestic and foreign policy and include both economic and political elements. This can create a tension in balancing various policy priorities, particularly for those policymakers who may support the TPP on some grounds but not others. Some opponents of the agreement argue that focusing on the strategic elements of the TPP distracts the debate from what they view should be its main criteria: the agreement's potential impact on the

U.S. economy. While both TPP critics and supporters cite different estimates of economic outcomes to support their positions, the broader strategic implications are highlighted largely by proponents, and can be difficult to quantify despite their potential significance.[14]

Economic Significance[15]

Preferential multi-country trade agreements, such as the TPP, generally are expected to alter trade relations among the participants by lowering tariffs on traded goods and by reducing nontariff barriers within countries. Most economists agree that reducing trade barriers enhances productivity by allocating resources towards their most efficient uses, increases consumer choice and lowers costs, stimulates economic growth, and at the national level improves economic welfare. The Japanese government, for example, hopes to use increased international competition achieved by TPP to revitalize its less productive sectors, including agriculture and services, and lower costs for consumers.[16] The gains of trade, however, are not necessarily distributed equally throughout an economy, and the resource reallocation that can lead to efficiency and job gains in some sectors may reduce production in other industries and can cause worker dislocation and job losses, a concern for policymakers and workers and firms in certain industries.[17]

Removing formal barriers to trade, primarily tariffs and quotas, directly lowers the price of traded goods. For example, the 20% tariff on certain Vietnamese-made shoes imported into the United States would be eliminated, while U.S.-grown walnuts would receive a 10% tariff discount in Japan, once eliminated. In turn, lower prices may impact trade patterns by increasing the overall amount of trade that occurs (trade creation) and by shifting trade away from countries that are not party to the agreement to those that are in the agreement (trade diversion). At times, countries are motivated to participate in trade agreements to prevent this type of trade diversion.

The magnitude of the trade creation and trade diversion effects that arise from TPP likely will be affected by a number of factors, including: the difference between pre-and post-agreement tariff rates, the speed with which tariff cuts are implemented, and a range of other external economic factors that affect global trade as a whole. For instance, the 2008-2010 global economic slowdown and the sharp drop in commodity prices and changes in exchange rates from 2014-2016 arguably had a greater impact on the volume of global trade and trade flows between countries than any FTA trade liberalization measures that might have gone into effect during this period. In addition, the impact of tariff cuts under the TPP may be muted to some extent due to the multiplicity of trade agreements that already exist among the participants and the already low tariff rates that are characteristic of trade among a number of the participants. (See "Tariffs" section below for more detail.)

In addition to the economic effects expected to result from cuts in tariffs, the TPP may offer long- term benefits to bilateral and regional trade through changes in domestic nontariff barriers that form the structure under which trade is conducted. In broad terms, the TPP incorporates rules and disciplines for open, nondiscriminatory treatment for participants. These rules are expected to reduce market-distorting activities that not only may reduce the overall level of trade, but also may create market distortions and inefficiencies. Analysts have indicated that some TPP participants, such as Vietnam, may use the rules and disciplines incorporated in the TPP to support a market-oriented reform agenda within their economies.[18] To the extent that countries undertake such reforms, the TPP could provide long-term economic benefits to the countries themselves and to other TPP participants. Other rules such as aspects of IPR protections and certain labor and environmental commitments are, in effect, less about economic openness and more about ensuring economic activity meets certain requirements. As such, the rationale behind them (i.e., encouraging innovation, protecting worker rights, and safeguarding the environment) can differ from the traditional economic arguments for trade liberalization.

TPP ECONOMIC IMPACT PREDICTIONS

A critical aspect of the debate on the TPP is the agreement's potential economic impact on countries both within and outside its current membership. The U.S. International Trade Commission (USITC) released a study on May 18, 2016, as required by TPA, to estimate the effect of the agreement on individual sectors in the U.S. economy.[19] The study uses a computable general equilibrium (CGE) model, working at the microeconomic level to estimate adjustments in consumption and production decisions in response to price changes. CGE models are a standard tool for estimating the impact of tariff changes. TPP commitments, however, include complex provisions that affect a broad array of issues going beyond just tariff schedules.

While the USITC study also attempts to measure the impact of changes in non-tariff barriers (NTBs), precisely modeling such changes is a challenge, requiring estimations in order to quantify both the existing NTBs and the rate and degree of their removal. Economic models by their nature, require simplification from the actual economic activity they attempt to represent and should be interpreted with careful consideration of their underlying assumptions and methodology. Below we examine the estimates from the USITC and other recent studies on the TPP.

USITC Study

Like most CGE models, the USITC study uses the Global Trade Analysis Project (GTAP) database hosted by Purdue University for its baseline data and projections. The study compares a scenario with the TPP provisions in effect relative to a projected baseline with no TPP, focusing largely on 2032 when most commitments would be phased in. Overall the study predicts a small positive benefit for the U.S. economy from participation in TPP in 2032 relative to the baseline—a 0.15% increase in GDP ($42.7 billion) and a 0.07% increase in employment (128,200 full time equivalents). The study breaks down its analysis by sectors, with agriculture and services sectors predicted to grow both in output (0.5% and 0.1%, respectively) and employment (0.5% and 0.1%, respectively). Output and employment in the manufactured goods, natural resources, and energy sector is estimated to decline slightly from the baseline (-0.1% and -0.2%, respectively) as TPP is expected to shift resources towards services and agriculture production.

Peterson Institute for International Economics Study

This study by Peter Petri and Michael Plummer is notable partly for its attempt to model liberalization of nontariff barriers (including those applied to trade in services) using tariff-equivalency estimates.[20] These nontariff changes, which are the most difficult to model precisely, drive the results of the study, with changes in tariffs accounting for only 12% of the economic benefits of the agreement—a point critics emphasize when questioning the validity of the study's results.[21] The Peterson study also estimates modest net gains for the United States and other TPP partners.

Small net losses are anticipated for some countries not participating in TPP including mainland China, India, South Korea, the Philippines, Thailand, and Indonesia. By 2030, the authors project the United States will see real annual income gains of about $131 billion above a baseline projection (or 0.5% above baseline GDP). These gains will not be spread uniformly throughout the economy, according to the model. The authors project some U.S. manufacturing industries to experience a drop in production from baseline, and the agriculture and any mining sectors to see a small increase. The service sector, however, is projected to see large relative gains, offsetting the negative impact on manufacturing. The model assumes TPP will not affect the overall level of employment, but may result in shifts from one sector to another. A January 2016 World Bank CGE analysis, prepared together with Petri and Plummer and based on a similar model, arrives at similar conclusions.[22] A complementary study from the Peterson Institute estimates the resultant adjustment costs from TPP induced-employment shifts.[23] Between 2017 and 2030, when the agreement is assumed phased in, the authors estimate total adjustment costs would be no more than 8% of TPP gains, providing ample means to compensate dislocated workers, potentially through an expanded Trade Adjustment Assistance program recommended by the authors.

Tufts Global Development and Environment Institute Study

Using nonstandard trade models, other researchers have produced studies suggesting the TPP will have overall negative effects on the U.S. and other economies. For example, a study published by the Global Development and Environment Institute at Tufts University projects the United States to experience a 0.54% reduction in GDP from baseline estimates by 2025, as well as the loss of 448,000 jobs from a baseline employment level.[24] In this study, all TPP participants are predicted to incur net employment losses due to the agreement, a result that runs counter to international trade theory, leading some economists to argue the methodology is ill-suited to examine a trade agreement.[25]

TPP would be significant among U.S. trade agreements, due to its size and the commitments reached. TPP would be the largest U.S. FTA by the number of parties and trade flows, though the majority of that trade is with countries with an existing U.S. FTA (**Figure 2**). Japan's participation has greatly increased the potential economic significance of the agreement. Among the

U.S. negotiating partners in the TPP, Japan is the largest economy and largest trading partner without an existing U.S. FTA (and hence, with greater scope for trade liberalization with the United States). In 2015, Japan was the United States' fourth largest goods export ($63 billion) and import ($131 billion) market.

Malaysia and Vietnam also stand out among the TPP countries without existing U.S. FTAs, both in terms of their current trade and investment with the United States and their potential for future growth. Both countries have young, relatively large populations (above 30 million in Malaysia and 90 million in Vietnam) and their economies have experienced rapid growth in recent years.[26] Moreover, Malaysia's and Vietnam's average applied most-favored nation tariffs—the average tariff on imports—are 6.1% and 9.5%, respectively, two of the highest levels among TPP members. Removal of various nontariff barriers in both countries is also a primary U.S. goal. Both nations also have substantial state sectors, which may be affected by TPP outcomes.

U.S.-TPP and FTA Trade Statistics

- TPP countries collectively represent the largest U.S. trading partner, accounting for 41% of total U.S. goods trade in 2015 and 23% of total U.S. services trade in 2014;[27]
- U.S. FTAs already exist with 6 U.S. trading partners among TPP participants, which account for 81% of U.S. goods trade with TPP partners in 2015 and 69% of U.S.-TPP services trade in 2014; and
- TPP countries together with all existing U.S. FTA partners, and the European Union, which is currently negotiating an FTA with the United States, account for 66% of U.S. goods trade. China accounts for nearly half of all U.S. goods trade with countries not currently negotiating or without an existing U.S. FTA.

U.S.-TPP Trade and Investment[28]

U.S. trade with TPP countries was more than $1.5 trillion in merchandise in 2015 and more than $276 billion in services in 2014, the most recent periods for which data are available (**Table A-1** and **Table A-2**, in Appendix). The flow of U.S. foreign direct investment (FDI) into TPP countries totaled

$61 billion in 2014, while TPP countries invested nearly $59 billion in the United States (**Table A-3**). The TPP would become the largest U.S. FTA by trade flows (**Figure 3**).

The TPP group of 12 countries is diverse in population, geographic location, and economic development, and U.S. trade relations with the countries reflect this diversity. The major U.S. merchandise exports are fairly similar to most TPP countries and include motor vehicles and parts; petroleum and coal products; computer equipment, semiconductors, and electronic components; agriculture and construction machinery; and aircraft. However, the top U.S. merchandise imports vary greatly by country. Agriculture and natural resources products are key U.S. imports from Australia, Chile, New Zealand, and Peru, while apparel products are the main U.S. imports from Vietnam. Canada and Mexico are both major suppliers of crude oil to the United States, but they also supply manufactured products like motor vehicles and motor vehicle parts. U.S. imports from Malaysia and Singapore consist primarily of manufactured products such as computers, semiconductors, and electronic components. Motor vehicles and motor vehicle parts make up nearly 35% of U.S. goods imports from Japan.

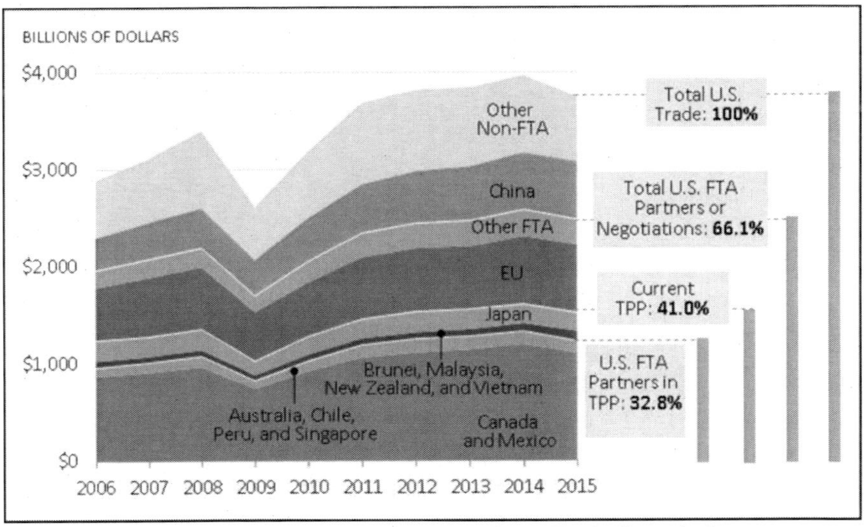

Source: CRS analysis. Data from the U.S. International Trade Commission.

Figure 2. U.S.-World, TPP, and FTA Partner Merchandise Trade.

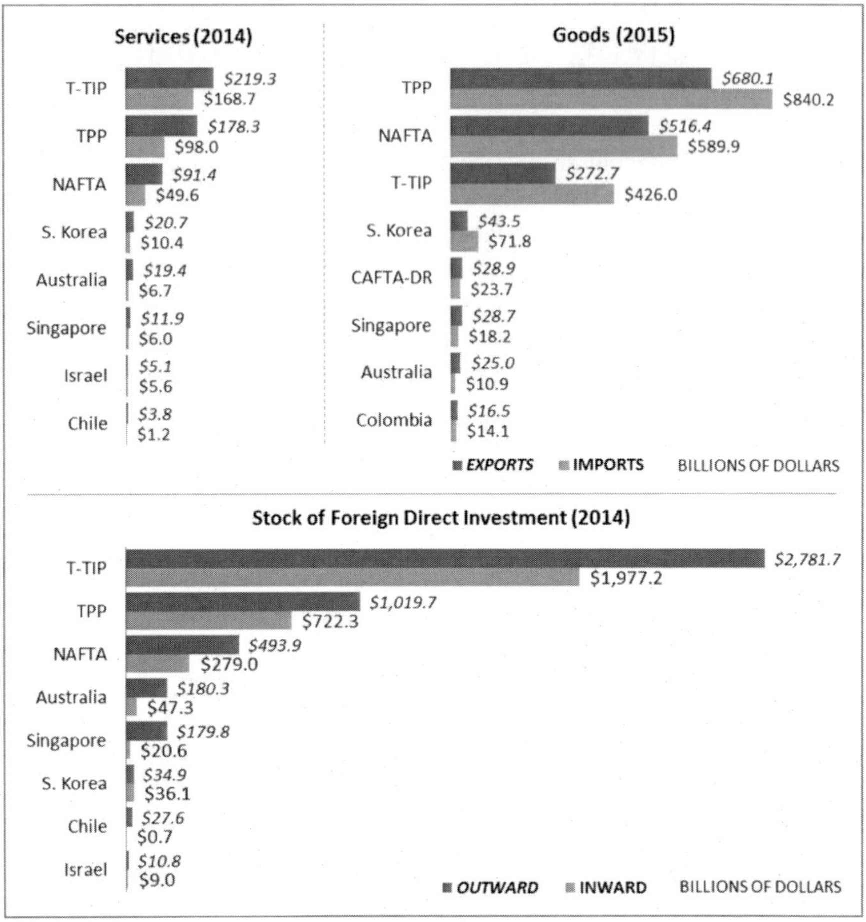

Source: Analysis by CRS. Data from BEA and USITC.

Notes: Services trade data not available for all FTA partners. T-TIP is the Trans-Atlantic Trade and Investment Partnership between the United States and European Union. CAFTA-DR is the U.S.-Central American- Dominican Republic FTA including Costa Rica, El Salvador, Guatemala, Honduras, and Nicaragua.

Figure 3. Largest U.S. FTAs.

In terms of value, Canada and Mexico are by far the largest U.S. trading partners among TPP countries in goods. Both countries share a long border with the United States and are among the oldest U.S. FTA partners. Japan is the third-largest U.S.-TPP goods trading partner, and second- largest services trade and investment partner. Among the other eight TPP partners, Singapore and Australia are the top U.S. goods export markets and top overall services trade and investment partners with the United States, while Malaysia, Vietnam, and Singapore are the top sources of U.S. goods imports.

Relationship to Existing Trade Organizations and Agreements

TPP and the WTO

Though designed as a regional trade agreement, the TPP could have a number of implications for the multilateral trading system represented by the WTO. Fundamentally, the proliferation of FTAs over the past two decades calls into question the multilateral system's ability to negotiate and implement new trade disciplines and further international trade liberalization.

Although WTO members agreed to a number of customs-related commitments as part of the Trade Facilitation Agreement in 2013, the goal of concluding a major multilateral trade round remains elusive nearly 15 years after the launch of the Doha Development Agenda negotiations in November 2001. Persistent differences among members about the extent and balance of trade liberalization continue to stymie progress in this forum and major issues, such as services trade liberalization are being negotiated among a subset of WTO members outside the body. The United States has pushed for the Doha Round to end and to be replaced by a more attainable package, but at the most recent WTO Ministerial in Nairobi, trade ministers were unable to agree on declaring an end to the Doha agenda, since developing countries fear that abandoning the Doha agenda may result in agricultural issues receiving less priority.

The last major round of global trade negotiations—the Uruguay Round—was concluded in 1994. Since then, global commerce has adapted to rapid advances in technology, with the result that current multilateral trade rules do not address some critical aspects of today's trading environment, including digital trade and e-commerce. New trade patterns have emerged and new obstacles to the flow of goods and services have appeared. This has left countries, including the United States, to pursue new or advanced trade rules and further liberalization through bilateral and regional agreements like the TPP.

Debate continues over whether or not bilateral and now "mega-regional" trade agreements help or hinder broader multilateral initiatives. On one hand, "mega-regionals," such as the TPP or the Trans-Atlantic Trade and Investment Partnership (T-TIP) negotiations between the United States and the European Union, could serve as alternative venues for establishing new rules and disciplines for the trading regime, and their size and economic significance could help spur negotiations at the multilateral level, influencing their direction. Some argue, for example, that the conclusion of the North American Free Trade Agreement (NAFTA), among the United States, Canada, and Mexico, effective since 1994, did in fact push the multilateral Uruguay Round negotiations to conclusion.[29]

On the other hand, if the locus of trade negotiations primarily shifts to "mega-regional" agreements, it could limit the overall effectiveness of the multilateral system. If the rules of the WTO no longer reflect the standards of trade policy to which much of the world has evolved, it could endanger the legitimacy of the organization in other aspects of its work, such as dispute settlement. A two-tier trading system, one working on more extensive rules and disciplines and one essentially dormant, could raise tensions by alienating those countries that feel they had no part in developing the new rules. Overlapping in membership with differing rules, these "mega- regional" agreements and other trade agreements could also add to the complexity of engaging in international commerce, as opposed to rules established at the WTO, which are applicable to nearly all world trading partners. They could also reduce economic efficiency in the global trading system if trade is diverted into these trading blocs due to preferential tariff treatment.

The TPP and Other Asia-Pacific Trade Agreements

The current 12 TPP countries form part of a growing network of Asia-Pacific FTAs (**Figure 4**). All TPP countries have at least one FTA with a TPP partner country, although the extent of trade liberalization varies among them. The United States has FTAs with six TPP countries, including Australia, Canada, Chile, Mexico, Peru, and Singapore. Four TPP countries—Brunei, Malaysia, Singapore, and Vietnam—are part of the Association of Southeast Asian Nations (ASEAN), which has a free trade area among its membership as well as several external FTAs.[30]

New FTAs involving key markets in the region have been concluded in recent years. For example, Australia recently implemented FTAs with China, Japan, and South Korea, and the European Union has concluded FTAs with Canada, and, most recently, Vietnam. As tariffs fall for the countries party to these agreements, it could put U.S. firms at a disadvantage in those markets without existing U.S. FTAs. This is the idea of "competitive liberalization" in practice, whereby new trade agreements spur other countries to enter into similar pacts in order to maintain their firms' competiveness in foreign markets. If the TPP were to enter into force, such motivation would likely be a major factor in drawing other countries' interest in joining the agreement.

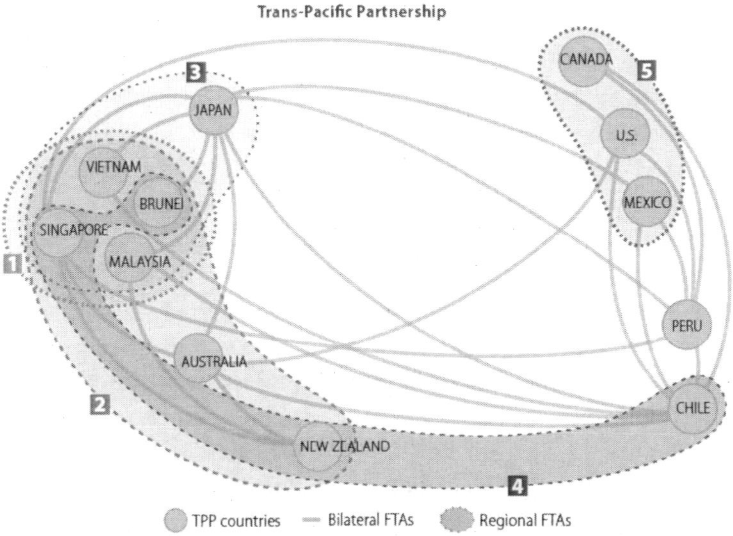

Encompassed Regional Trade Agreements

	1 ASEAN	2 ASEAN-AUSTRALIA-NZ	3 ASEAN-JAPAN	4 P-4	5 NAFTA
Australia		■			
Brunei	■	■	■	■	
Canada					■
Chile				■	
Japan			■		
Malaysia	■	■	■		
Mexico					■
New Zealand		■		■	
Peru					
Singapore	■	■	■	■	
United States					■
Vietnam	■	■	■		

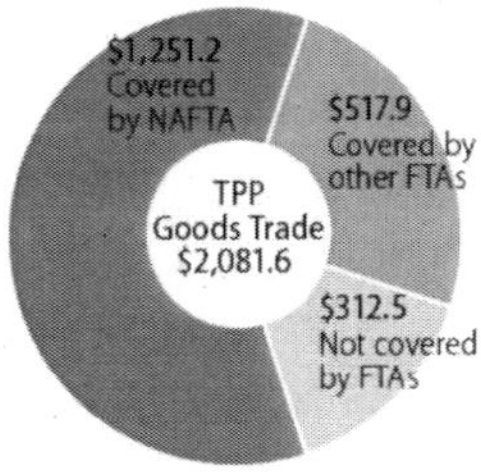

($Billions, 2014. "Other FTAs" includes trade between Japan and Australia, though Japan-Australia FTA wasn't in effect until 2015.)

Source: WTO FTA database and websites of TPP countries' trade ministries. Trade data from IMF.

Notes: Aggregate TPP goods trade, both imports and exports, as reported above. ASEAN also includes countries outside the TPP: Burma (Myanmar), Cambodia, Indonesia, Laos, the Philippines, and Thailand. TPP goods trade covered by existing FTAs, as depicted above, reflects all goods trade between FTA partners. This measure slightly overstates trade covered under FTAs, as most FTAs exclude market access for some goods.

Figure 4. Existing FTAs among TPP Countries.

All 12 TPP partners are also members of the Asia-Pacific Economic Cooperation (APEC) forum, which does not negotiate FTAs but serves as a forum for dialogue on, and establishes nonbinding commitments toward, the goals of open trade and investment within the region.[31] In the context of this forum for dialogue and nonbinding commitments, APEC Leaders have repeatedly agreed to push forward the creation of a Free Trade Area of the Asia-Pacific (FTAAP).

Twelve countries in APEC, seven of which are also in TPP, are currently negotiating the Regional Comprehensive Economic Partnership Agreement (RCEP). ASEAN leads the negotiations for this proposed FTA among its members and six ASEAN FTA partners (Australia, China, India, Japan, New Zealand, and South Korea).[32] Both the RCEP and the TPP would encompass a significant share of regional economic activity, but each currently includes only one of the region's two economic leaders, the United States and China. The breadth and depth of trade liberalization resulting from two potential agreements is likely to differ. In their 2015 Declaration, APEC Leaders recognized both the TPP and the RCEP, which includes China, but not the United States, as "ongoing regional undertakings" on which to eventually achieve an FTAAP.[33]

As noted above, the TPP could not enter into force without the United States and Japan. It is conceivable, however, that the other 11 countries, after spending five years negotiating an agreement not only with the United States, but among themselves as well, could conclude a replacement agreement without the United States. It would not have the economic heft of an agreement with the United States, but it still would contain the third-largest economy (Japan) and could serve as a vehicle for further Asian integration.

CORE PROVISIONS

The text of the TPP agreement spans 30 chapters. The main goal as stated by the negotiating countries is "to establish a comprehensive, next-generation regional agreement that liberalizes trade and investment and addresses new and traditional trade issues and 21st-century challenges."[34] FTA provisions are often discussed in two different categories: (1) the market access component addressing tariff and nontariff barriers to trade in goods, services, and agriculture, and government procurement; and (2) the rules component covering the procedures, standards, and regulatory considerations that relate to international trade, including such issues as investment and intellectual property rights. Market access can be affected by the process by which trade is conducted, and, hence, the distinction between these two categories is not always clear. While tariff negotiations are perhaps the most well-known component of trade agreements and the easiest to measure and verify, U.S. firms are often most competitive in the international trade of services and products involving high levels of research and development. These industries face mostly nontariff, behind-the-border barriers, making rules commitments such as transparent regulatory procedures or IPR protection particularly important for U.S. access to and ability to compete in overseas markets.

U.S. FTAs also attempt to ensure that U.S. FTA partners meet certain requirements. In particular, internationally-recognized and other core principles for the protection of worker rights and the environment have become a significant aspect of U.S. trade agreement negotiations. In addition, the TPP includes an entirely new chapter that seeks to establish disciplines on how state-owned enterprises engage in international trade, with a goal of limiting potential negative impacts on private actors from nonmarket practices.

The 12 TPP countries have varying competitive advantages, sensitivities, and levels of economic development. As a result of these differences and the "give and take" of trade negotiations, achieving common TPP rules and disciplines also involves certain exceptions in different forms, and phase-in periods of varying lengths. When examining the specific commitments of the agreement it is important to examine these exceptions, as they may impact the agreement's practical application.

This section examines the major issues addressed in the TPP negotiations, beginning with the treatment of trade in merchandise goods. For each issue the report provides background information, a discussion of the provisions in the text, particularly as they relate to previous trade agreements, and a summary of the debate on the topic, including, where relevant, U.S. trade negotiating objectives.

Stakeholders' views on the TPP agreement vary. Some groups generally oppose or support trade liberalization; others' positions hinge on specific provisions in the TPP text. Most business groups generally support the agreement, while most labor unions and certain nongovernmental organizations (NGOs) are generally opposed.[35] The discussion that follows focuses on specific commitments in the agreement and debate over those measures.

Goods

Although services are an increasingly important aspect of international trade, physical goods still account for the bulk of such activity. In 2015, merchandise trade accounted for over 75% of the nearly $5 trillion in U.S. trade. Expanding opportunities for trade in goods by reducing and eliminating tariff and nontariff barriers remains a top priority for U.S. trade negotiations, highlighted by Congress in its first principal negotiating objective in the TPA-2015.

Tariffs[36]

Background

Like previous U.S. FTAs, TPP would eventually eliminate all industrial goods tariffs and most agriculture tariffs and quotas. These commitments would be phased in over varying periods. For some of the most sensitive agriculture products, tariff and quota protections would remain in place or only be partially removed. Each of the 12 TPP countries has its own unique tariff schedule laying out its product-specific tariff commitments.[37] These schedules list each country's individual tariff lines (i.e., a list of products described by Harmonized Tariff Schedule (HTS) product codes at the 8-10 digit level of aggregation) and include the current tariff rate (base rate), the relevant staging category, and the post-TPP annual tariff rates.[38]

The staging categories explain the speed and scope of tariff elimination for a specific product. For example, "entry-into-force" signifies a removal of that product's tariff immediately when the agreement becomes effective. The categories may be simple, such as an annual equal decrease until the tariff is eliminated, or more complex, such as staying at current levels for a period of years before decreasing by varying amounts. The United States has 36 unique staging categories that apply to its tariff commitments, surpassed only by Japan, which has 60. The United States has the longest phase-out period of any TPP country, and longer than any previous U.S. FTA; it would delay the complete removal of tariffs on light trucks from Japan, for example, and certain dairy products from New Zealand for 30 years.[39]

While most TPP countries negotiated a single TPP tariff schedule with their partners, the United States negotiated bilaterally such that for certain import-sensitive products, U.S. tariff and quota commitments differ by partners. As a result, U.S. tariffs on some products may be eliminated according to different staging categories for different countries. This bilateral approach to tariff commitments within a multi-party agreement stands in contrast to the most-favored nation (MFN) approach in the WTO, which achieves a single tariff schedule for all trading partners. U.S. negotiators argue that this bilateral approach allows for more complete liberalization overall, but some observers question this assertion and raise concerns over setting this precedent for multi- party negotiations.[40]

Key factors impacting the potential significance of TPP tariff commitments include the following:

- **Current Tariff Levels.** Average MFN applied tariff rates among TPP countries currently range from 0.2% in Singapore to 9.5% in Vietnam (Appendix 1). Given the already low simple U.S. average tariff rate (3.5%), U.S. rates would change less through TPP than those for some other countries, especially Vietnam and Malaysia.
- **Existing Trade Agreements.** Each TPP country has existing FTAs with at least four other TPP countries, and Chile has existing FTAs with all 11 other TPP countries. In 2014, 85% of goods trade among TPP parties occurred between partners with existing trade agreements.[41] Depending on the degree of tariff liberalization in these existing agreements, the tariff commitments in TPP may not require a significant adjustment for some TPP parties. For example, under NAFTA, the United States, Canada, and Mexico have eliminated nearly all tariffs on trade between the three countries. In cases where existing agreements offer different tariff rates than the TPP, exporters would be able to choose which agreement to utilize as long as they also met the relevant rules of origin.
- **Product Mix.** While tariffs are below 10% on average in all TPP countries, product-specific peaks can be much higher, above 100% on certain sensitive items. TPP tariff commitments may have a larger impact on countries that trade heavily in these high-tariff products. For example, U.S. imports from Vietnam are concentrated in high-tariff footwear and apparel products. U.S. exports facing relatively high tariffs in certain TPP markets include autos, agricultural products, and heavy machinery.
- **Effective Tariff Rates**. Calculated by dividing collected duties by the value of imports, this measure effectively incorporates the factors discussed above to provide an indication of the average duty actually paid on imports from a particular country. Among TPP countries, U.S.

effective duty rates in 2015 were highest on imports from Vietnam (**Figure 5**). Without readily available data on duties collected by other TPP countries, a similar calculation cannot be made for effective duty rates on U.S. exports.

Key Provisions with Non-U.S. FTA Countries

Given the existing U.S. FTAs with Australia, Canada, Chile, Mexico, Peru, and Singapore, which include comprehensive tariff coverage, this section focuses only on TPP tariff commitments between the United States and the five TPP countries without an existing U.S. FTA (Brunei, Japan, Malaysia, New Zealand, and Vietnam).[42]

Table 1. TPP Country Tariff and Trade Agreement Statistics

Country	MFN Average Applied Tariff (%)	Unique TPP Staging Categories	Longest TPP Phase-Out Period (Years)	Existing FTAs with TPP Partners	TPP Trade with Existing FTA Partners (%)
Australia	2.7	7	4	8	96.5
Brunei	1.2	10	11	6	93.0
Canada	4.2	7	12	4	95.0
Chile	6	3*	8	11	100.0
Japan	4.2	60	21	9	45.9
Malaysia	6.1	6	16	7	76.8
Mexico	7.5	20	16	5	97.9
New Zealand	2.0	4	7	6	54.7
Peru	3.4	6	16	6	96.4
Singapore	0.2	1	0	9	97.5
United States	3.5	36	30	6	82.0
Vietnam	9.5	36	21	7	57.8

Source: WTO Tariff Profiles, TPP tariff schedules, and IMF Direction of Trade Statistics.

Notes: (a) For a list of trade agreements among TPP countries see Appendix Table A-1 in CRS Report R42344, *Trans-Pacific Partnership (TPP) Countries: Comparative Trade and Economic Analysis*, by Brock R. Williams. (b) The number of staging categories excludes agriculture products covered under TRQs. (*) Chile's tariff schedule also includes 17 categories matching TPP commitments to commitments in its previous FTAs.

(2015)

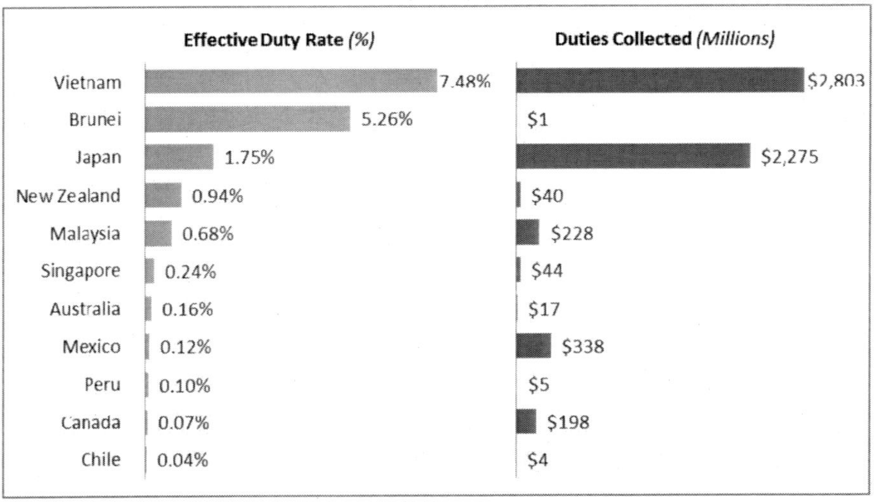

Source: Analysis by CRS. Data from USITC.

Notes: Effective duty rates calculated by dividing imports for consumption by collected duties.

Figure 5. U.S. Collected Duties and Effective Duty Rates.

Key aspects of TPP tariff commitments among these countries include (see **Figure 6**):

- More than one-third of tariff lines are already duty-free in each country: U.S. (37%), Brunei (76%), Japan (39%), Malaysia (65%), New Zealand (58%), and Vietnam (32%).
- Most tariff elimination would occur in the first years after the agreement's entry into force, with more than 80% of tariff lines duty-free in each country after three years, rising to approximately 90% after ten years.
- Eventually 95% or more tariff lines in each country would be duty-free. U.S. commitments would be phased in over the longest period, with tariff phase outs on two products up to 30 years after the agreement's entry into force, although on average U.S. tariff commitments are similar to the other countries.

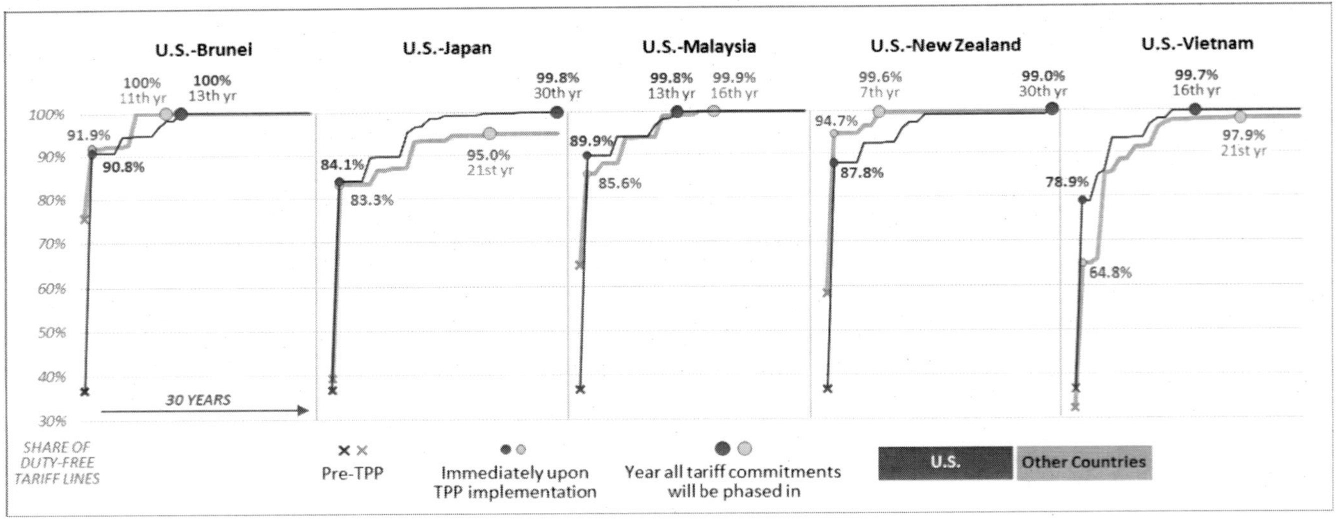

Source: CRS analysis of TPP tariff schedules.

Note: Japanese tariff commitments on more than 1% of tariff lines are of a complexity that required some judgement by the authors to determine whether they would be completely liberalized for U.S. products, including some cases with multiple tariffs associated with the same HTS code. In these cases, the authors' included only the least liberalized tariff in their calculations. Some HTS codes in the Japanese tariff schedule also appear to apply to only a subset of TPP countries. Those not applicable to the United States were excluded from the calculations. Finally, approximately 50 tariff lines in the Japanese schedule refer to non-originating goods, and were also excluded—this updated methodology from an earlier version of the report increased the share of Japanese tariff lines eventually becoming duty free from 94.4% to 95.0%.

Figure 6. TPP Tariff Commitments between the U. S. and Non-FTA Countries.

- In terms of U.S. exports, more than 99% of tariff lines would eventually be duty- free in Brunei, New Zealand and Malaysia. Japan and Vietnam would maintain some level of tariff protection on more than 2% of their tariff lines (approximately 200 lines in Vietnam, mostly agricultural products like sugar, as well as used autos, and more than 400 lines in Japan comprised mostly of agricultural products, including pork and dairy).
- In terms of U.S. imports, more than 99% of tariff lines would eventually be duty- free for all five countries. The United States would maintain tariffs on some products from each country, with the highest number of tariffs remaining on imports from New Zealand (approximately 100 tariff lines, mostly dairy products).
- These rates of duty elimination are similar to previous U.S. FTAs, but with somewhat longer phase out periods and a slightly higher share of tariff lines excluded from liberalization. For example, in the KORUS FTA, both South Korea and the United States committed to eventually eliminate duties on more than 99% of tariff lines, with more than 92% of tariff lines duty-free within five years.[43]

TPP Product-Specific Tariff Commitments: Illustrative Examples

U.S. Imports

Shoes. HS Code (6404.11.90) Current Tariff (20%)

In 2015, this type of athletic shoe was the top U.S. footwear import from TPP countries ($797 million). The current 20% U.S. import tariff on this type of shoe would be immediately eliminated for all TPP countries.

Light Trucks. HS Code (8704.31.00) Current Tariff (25%)

In 2015, the U.S. imported $12.8 billion in light trucks from TPP countries. Currently these imports come almost exclusively from Mexico, an existing U.S. FTA partner. Through TPP, the 25% light truck tariff would be eliminated immediately for the 6 current U.S. FTA partners (as is already the case under the bilateral agreements), and after ten years with ten equal annual reductions for the non-FTA partners, except for Japan. For Japan this tariff would remain at 25% until eliminated in year 30 of the agreement.

Luggage and Handbags. HS Code (4202) Current Tariff (0-20%)

In 2015, the U.S. imported $1.2 billion of luggage and handbags from TPP countries, primarily from Vietnam and Mexico. Tariffs are already eliminated for Mexico under NAFTA. Most U.S. tariffs on these products for other countries, currently as high as 20%, would be immediately eliminated, and all such tariffs would be eliminated by year 6 of the agreement.

U.S. Exports

Heavy Equipment - Malaysia. HS Code (8429) Current Tariff (5-25%)

In 2015, the United States exported $3.1 billion of heavy machinery (e.g., scrapers, bulldozers, graders) to all TPP countries, including $11 million to Malaysia. Under TPP, Malaysia would eliminate all tariffs on such equipment, currently as high as 25%, by year six of the agreement's entry into force.

Nuts - Japan. HS Code (0802.32.00) Current Tariff (10%)

In 2015, the United States exported $309 million of walnuts to TPP countries, including $116 million to Japan. Under

TPP, Japan would immediately eliminate the 10% tariff on imports of walnuts from the United States.

Motorcycles - Vietnam. HS Code (8711.50.20) Current Tariff (85%)

In 2015, the United States exported less than $1million of large-engine motorcycles to Vietnam, but more than $461 million to all TPP partners. Under TPP, Vietnam would eliminate the 85% tariff on these imports from the United States in eight annual stages.

Sources: U.S. trade data from the Census Bureau accessed through the ITC's trade dataweb. Tariff data from the official TPP tariff schedules.

Rules of Origin (ROO)[44]

Rules of origin (ROO) determine whether products "originate" within an FTA area and, therefore, are eligible to receive the benefits when imported into an FTA member state. Thus, they are used to ensure that the parties to an FTA receive the tariff liberalization benefits and to prevent transshipments. In practice, however, restrictive rules of origin can also be used to limit the impact of FTAs on import-sensitive sectors. In the TPP, as in other FTAs, rules of origin are laid out in detail in the agreement and would need to be approved by Congress as part of the implementing legislation.

All FTAs and preference programs have distinctive ROO, but the ways that they are developed are similar. One ROO type requires that a product illustrate that it is "substantially transformed" (i.e., made into a "new and distinct" product) by showing a "tariff shift," a change in its HTS tariff classification. The degree of change required varies by product. The "yarn forward" rule, a tariff-shift rule that is a guiding principle in TPP for textiles and apparel, requires that all qualifying products must be produced in the FTA region beginning with the yarn. Some product- specific ROO in TPP and other FTAs require that a minimum *ad valorem* (value) percentage of the product must be produced in the FTA region. TPP uses regional value content rules for many products, including automobiles, appliances, and machine tools. Another kind of ROO specifies that the value of foreign content must not exceed a certain maximum percentage (i.e., a *de minimis* rule, which in TPP is 10%). Third, ROO for some products require that some kind of manufacturing or processing operation (e.g., a chemical reaction) must be completed in the region.

TPP ROO allow for cumulation among TPP countries. This means a TPP country manufacturer can use unlimited inputs from other TPP partners and have the finished product qualify for TPP tariff benefits. This could provide an incentive for creation of new regional supply chains within the TPP area, and may encourage other countries to join the TPP to avoid being left out of supply chains.

For the majority of goods, the ROO in most U.S. FTAs, including TPP, are quite similar in most areas. However, TPP ROO pertaining to certain import-sensitive manufacturing industries, especially in the textile, apparel, and footwear sectors and the automotive industry, have important distinctions from previous FTAs (see below).

Textiles, Apparel, and Footwear[45]

Background

While the United States continues to produce certain yarns and fabrics, some of which are used in apparel production abroad, nearly all apparel sold in the United States is imported and most U.S.- headquartered apparel companies have limited or no U.S. manufacturing capabilities.[46] Instead, they rely on extensive global supply chains, which, in turn, depend on costs, lead times, and other considerations. As a result of these dynamics, the U.S. textile industry generally supported gradual TPP textile and apparel tariff reductions, but only if the imported products are assembled using yarn produced in a TPP country (i.e., the "yarn-forward" rule of origin). Meanwhile, trade organizations representing U.S. apparel companies and retailers generally supported the immediate elimination of textile and apparel tariffs upon implementation of the TPP agreement, opposing the yarn-forward rule of origin as too restrictive.

As with apparel products, most footwear consumed in the United States is imported from abroad, with import penetration in the industry well above 90%.[47] Over a decade ago, the U.S. footwear industry reached a general agreement supporting immediate elimination of nearly all footwear tariffs in future trade agreements, except for a number of sensitive items determined still to be manufactured in the United States.[48]

Vietnam has been a major focus of U.S. negotiations over TPP commitments on textile, apparel, and footwear. Vietnam accounted for 12% of apparel and 15% of footwear imported by the United States in 2015, and was the second-largest supplier of apparel and footwear to the United States after China.[49] It is the only large apparel and footwear producer among TPP partners without an existing FTA with the United States. Currently, Vietnam's apparel sector sources the overwhelming majority of its yarns and fabrics from non-TPP members, mainly China, Taiwan, and South Korea, and it purchases only a small amount of yarns and fabrics (about $100 million in 2015) from the United States.[50]

Although associations representing the U.S. textile industry ultimately support the TPP, domestic industry raised concerns over the potential for Vietnamese-made apparel displacing garments manufactured with U.S. fabric in Western Hemisphere countries such as Mexico, El Salvador, Honduras, and Nicaragua, where garment makers currently must use U.S. inputs to obtain duty- free access to the U.S. market under NAFTA and the U.S.-Central America-Dominican Republic FTA (CAFTA-DR).[51] They also raised concerns over Mexico and Peru, both TPP members, potentially shifting sourcing of textile inputs from the United States to Vietnam should it develop an industry that can produce large quantities of textiles.[52] On the other hand, proponents of FTAs as a tool for economic development would argue that encouraging movement up the value chain, such as from apparel to textile production, in a developing country like Vietnam is a goal of U.S. FTAs.

Textile, apparel, and footwear tariffs differ considerably among TPP countries.[53] The TPP countries currently face U.S. tariff rates as high as 25% on textiles, 32% on apparel, and up to nearly 50% on footwear. Other TPP countries also maintain high tariffs, including Vietnam, whose apparel tariffs range from 5% to 20%.

USITC Estimated Economic Impact

The USITC, in its May 2016 report on the economic impact of TPP, estimated sector-specific outcomes for textiles and apparel, and footwear.[54] Their study, which compares a TPP scenario in 2032 against a non-TPP baseline, estimated that the apparel industry would see an increase in imports over the 2032 baseline of 1.4% or $1.9 billion, and a smaller increase in exports of 0.3% or $10 million. Vietnam would account for much of this import growth, while imports from China would be expected to decline. Textile imports and exports would also be expected to increase over the baseline, by 1.6% ($869 million) and 1.3% ($257 million), respectively. The study estimated output and employment slightly above the baseline for the apparel industry (an increase of 1.0% and 0.9%, respectively), and slightly below for textiles (a decrease of 0.4% for both output and employment). Regarding footwear, USITC estimated a slight overall rise in total U.S. imports of 2.7% or $1.1 billion, but a major shift in sourcing toward TPP countries with imports from the region increasing by 23.4% or $1.6 billion. As most U.S. footwear is already imported, the agreement is not expected to have a significant impact on the U.S. industry, although the study estimated an increase above baseline in exports to Vietnam, mostly in intermediate components, and shows a slight (0.5%) increase in U.S. footwear output.

Key Provisions

Tariffs. All textile, apparel, and footwear tariffs will either be eliminated immediately or phased out in various stages over a decade or more following implementation of the TPP agreement. The United States has eight different tariff phase out schedules for textiles, apparel, and footwear. The longest phase out periods apply to the most sensitive products, such as certain men's and boys' overcoats, some women's and girls' blouses and skirts, men's leather boots and work shoes, and women's pumps. Tariffs on these products will be fully eliminated at the end of year 10 or 12, after an initial reduction of 50% or 55% when the pact enters into force.

Safeguard. Like most U.S. FTAs, the TPP includes a textile and apparel safeguard that will allow the United States to reimpose tariffs if import surges cause or threaten to cause serious damage to domestic industry. This option will be available for five years after the agreement enters into force, and each safeguard action may last for two years with a possible two-year extension. In addition, the United States may unilaterally suspend future tariff phase outs after five years of implementation if it determines that Vietnam has failed to allow independent unions and grant them the right to strike by that time (see below section on labor provisions).[55]

Rules of Origin. To qualify for favorable tariff treatment, textiles and apparel must meet a yarn- forward rule of origin, which requires the use of U.S. or other TPP country yarns and fabrics, with only a few exceptions, in textile and apparel products traded within the TPP area.[56] Footwear manufacturers can qualify their shoes as TPP-originated under (1) a tariff shift method, requiring that sufficient production occurred entirely within the TPP region to change the tariff classification of the goods, or (2) one of two different methods of measuring the share of a product's value that was added within the TPP region.[57] These ROO may give Vietnamese producers of footwear an advantage in the U.S. market over producers in other Asian countries that do not benefit from tariff preferences.

Short Supply List. Like other U.S. FTAs with a yarn-forward rule of origin for textiles and apparel, the TPP provides an exception for products that are deemed to be in "short supply" within the TPP region. The TPP short supply list includes 187 fibers, yarns, and fabrics, such as cashmere, certain wool yarns for sweaters, and polyester/wool blend fabrics.[58] The agreement would allow goods made within the TPP region using non-TPP inputs from the short supply list to qualify for privileged access when exported to other TPP countries.[59] Other exceptions to the textile and apparel ROO allow synthetic knit and woven baby clothes and brassieres cut and sewn in other TPP countries to be exported to the United States even if the yarn and fabric are not produced within the TPP region.

Earned Import Allowance. The TPP pact includes a program called the Earned Import Allowance Program to encourage the use of American fabrics in Vietnamese-manufactured jeans and khaki pants. The provision exempts some U.S. apparel imports from Vietnam from the TPP yarn-forward rule provided Vietnam imports a specific quantity of U.S. fabrics. This would allow a limited amount of apparel cut, sewn, and assembled in Vietnam to enter the United States duty- free even if the garments include fabric from non-TPP countries.[60]

Importantly, because both the ROO and the Earned Import Allowance program are complex and have substantial compliance and reporting requirements, some manufacturers in previous FTAs have opted to simply pay import duties rather than prove a product meets the specified requirements.[61]

Customs Enforcement and Implementation. The TPP includes specific customs procedures to enforce each TPP country's commitments, such as visiting textile and apparel factories to conduct verification activities. A Committee on Textile and Apparel Matters is to be established under the TPP, where industry can raise concerns and issues can be resolved on trade in these products.

Industry Views

The Industry Trade Advisory Committee (ITAC) on Textiles and Clothing (ITAC 13) summarizes the industry's divergent views.[62] Committee members generally applauded the greater opening of global markets, but they differed sharply "over how that should be accomplished, whether that involves greater U.S. market access for foreign products, and what role consumer perspectives should play in this debate."[63] There were also strong differences over how the trade negotiations could best accommodate industry adjustments to additional competition. The National Council of Textile Organizations (NCTO), the industry group representing the domestic textile industry, [64] the American Apparel and Footwear Association (AAFA), the national trade association of the apparel and nonrubber footwear industries, and the Footwear Distributors and Retailers of America[65] have endorsed the TPP. In contrast, Patagonia, an apparel retailer, has stated its opposition to the TPP, as has New Balance, a footwear company that maintains some production in the United States.[66]

Motor Vehicles[67]

Background

The United States and Japan are the second- and third-largest auto manufacturing nations, respectively, which made motor vehicle market access issues central to the TPP negotiations (**Table 2**). Other TPP signatories that produce motor vehicles are Canada, Mexico, Malaysia, and Vietnam. Japan, Mexico, the United States, and Canada all export large numbers of vehicles. As a result of market forces and the elimination of vehicle trade barriers in NAFTA, the North American auto industry has become highly integrated. The largest source of U.S. imports from outside the NAFTA region is Japan, which shipped over 1.5 million vehicles to the United States in 2014.[68]

U.S. vehicle exports have steadily risen since the 2007-2009 recession and exports to other TPP countries could grow further as tariffs fall and nontariff barriers (NTBs) are reduced or eliminated.[69] In 2014, U.S. vehicle exports exceeded two million units for the first time, having doubled since 2009.

Nearly half of those exports were sold in Canada (870,025 units). Other TPP destinations for U.S. vehicle exports were Mexico (151,902), Australia (61,052), Japan (19,003), Chile (16,631), Peru (6,354), and New Zealand (5,013).[70] However, while TPP markets accounted for 56% of U.S. vehicle exports to the world,[71] most of those exports already benefit from duty- free access under various regional and bilateral trade agreements. Japan is the only large vehicle market among TPP countries that is not covered by an FTA with the United States.

TPA-2015 did not spell out specific TPP objectives for trade in motor vehicles. Rather, motor vehicle industry goals were subsumed under general objectives to reduce tariffs and NTBs and to refrain from foreign currency manipulation. TPP auto manufacturing countries sought the elimination or reduction of U.S. vehicle tariffs, which are currently 2.5% on passenger vehicles and 25% on pick-up trucks. A related goal was to develop rules of origin for TPP vehicle trade that would ensure parts supply chains could operate smoothly but with strong verification and enforcement procedures. Some of the rules for vehicle trade in NAFTA and the U.S.-South Korea FTA (KORUS) served as reference points for TPP negotiators.

USITC Estimated Economic Impact

The USITC study estimated impacts on the passenger vehicle industry over 30 years given the long phaseout period for tariffs in this sector.[72] The study highlights three significant periods during this transition: (1) after year 6, Canada, the top U.S. export market, would eliminate tariffs on imports from Japan potentially increasing competition for U.S. auto producers in that market; (2) by year 13 Malaysia and Vietnam would eliminate auto import duties, making U.S. exports more competitive in those markets; and (3) by year 30 the United States would eliminate its import tariffs on Japanese autos potentially increasing competition in the U.S. market for U.S. producers. Ultimately, the study predicts an increase from the 2047 baseline in vehicle and parts exports of 2% ($2.9 billion) and 1.5% ($2.1 billion), respectively. Imports are expected to be above baseline by 1.1% ($4.3 billion) for vehicles and 1.5% ($4.5 billion) for parts. Relative to the baseline, output and employment are expected to increase slightly for autos (2% for each), and decline slightly for parts (-0.2% for output and -0.3% for employment).

Table 2. TPP Signatories with Vehicle Production

2015		
Country	**Units Produced**	**Units Sold Domestically**
United States	12,100,095	17,470,659
Japan	9,278,238	5,562,887
Mexico	3,565,469	1,351,648
Canada	2,283,474	1,939,949
Malaysia	614,671	666,674
Vietnam	50,000	209,804

Source: International Organization of Motor Vehicle Manufacturers, www.oica.net.
Notes: Vehicles include passenger cars and commercial vehicles.

Key Provisions

Tariffs. If the TPP agreement comes into force, member countries will eventually eliminate import tariffs on most vehicles and parts. U.S. tariff commitments, including for motor vehicles, are on a bilateral basis, so tariff reduction speeds differ with respect to each country.[73] The longest tariff phaseouts are applied to vehicle shipments from Japan to the United States. In that case, the 2.5% tariff on passenger cars will remain in place until year 15, after which it will be eliminated gradually through year 25 after the agreement's entry into force. The 25% U.S. light truck tariff with Japan is not phased out, but eliminated only in year 30 of the TPP. The U.S. rationale for longer tariff phase outs on Japanese vehicles than on those from other countries is that a longer transition is necessary for Japan to remove its own NTBs and move toward a "more open automotive market."[74] The reduction in foreign barriers to U.S. vehicles is likely to be most significant in Malaysia and Vietnam, where current high tariff levels make imported vehicles costly. Malaysia's vehicle tariffs are as much as 40%; Vietnam's as much as 70%.

Nontariff Barriers. NTBs in the vehicle industry fall into two categories: (1) suppression of imports through tax breaks for local vehicles and local content requirements for domestically produced cars and parts; and (2) safety and environmental regulations that limit vehicle trade because the regulatory requirements differ among countries.[75] Although Japan does not assess tariffs on vehicles, its consistently low level of vehicle imports has led to assertions that NTBs are used to restrict sale of foreign-made vehicles. Bilateral U.S.-Japan side letters to the TPP agreement establish a special joint dispute resolution process and commit Japan to

- adopt a more open automotive rulemaking process;
- accept a limited number of U.S. motor vehicle safety regulations on an equivalency basis with similar Japanese standards;
- reduce barriers to establishing vehicle distribution centers; and
- apply financial incentives equally to imported as well as domestic vehicles.[76]

Rules of Origin. The motor vehicle rules of origin, while focused to some extent on U.S.-Japan vehicle trade, are also of interest to Canada and Mexico, which seek to maintain their own large auto-making industries in the face of increased competition from Asian production. The NAFTA rules served as a model for the TPP. To receive reduced tariffs under NAFTA, 62.5% of a vehicle's content must be manufactured in the United States, Canada, or Mexico. The NAFTA net cost method takes total vehicle manufacturing costs, then subtracts costs of promotion, marketing, shipping and other factors. The resulting figure is then divided into the value of regional content—determined by subtracting the value of all the parts originating outside of the NAFTA area from the net cost—to find the percentage of regional content. In its own bilateral trade agreements, however, Japan has used a different calculation, known as the build-down method, and it argued that this should be the basis of vehicle rules of origin in the TPP. The build-down method does not subtract shipping and marketing before making the regional content determination, so cars using this method would have higher regional content than if the net cost method were used. The formula in the TPP allows either approach, requiring vehicles to have 45% TPP content using the net cost method or 55% using the build-down method to qualify for tariff preferences. The 45% net cost RVC in TPP is lower than the 62.5% level in NAFTA, but above the 35% level in KORUS.

Vehicle and parts manufacturers producing and exporting within North America would be able to choose whether to use the NAFTA or TPP rules of origin. While the rules of origin differential between NAFTA and TPP may not impact vehicle trade, it may affect trade in auto parts. That is because the required TPP share of value for auto parts to receive preferential treatment is significantly lower than the threshold for vehicles, ranging from 35% to 45%, depending on the type of accounting used. While different regional value content standards for vehicles and parts were used in NAFTA—62.5% for vehicles and 60% for parts—the standards were closer than they are in TPP.[77] Under TPP rules, some auto parts whose value was added mainly outside the TPP region may be able to enter the United States duty-free. This differential led ITAC 2 to note that its auto industry members "acknowledge the real concerns raised by some that the automotive origin RVC [regional value content] is not sufficiently strong, particularly for automotive parts."[78]

Industry Views

The motor vehicle industry does not have a unified position on the TPP; some automakers support it,[79] others have raised concerns,[80] and one company opposes it.[81] The United Autoworkers union (UAW) opposes it.[82] Concerns include the following:

- ***Currency Manipulation.*** Some automakers (as well as some other manufacturers) recommended that the TPP include an enforceable commitment to prohibit currency manipulation. Instead, the TPP establishes a Macroeconomic Policy Authority Forum (see below section on currency), which the International Trade Advisory Committee for autos (ITAC 2) says falls short of its recommendations, but which "could help mitigate the misuse of exchange rate policies and the adverse economic impact this policy practice has had on the United States...."[83]
- ***U.S.-Japan Side Letters and Appendix.*** ITAC 2 considers Japan's vehicle NTB commitments as marginal improvements, but expects that they "will not lead to a substantially larger U.S. presence in the Japanese motor vehicle market."[84] It contends that these commitments are not enforceable under the TPP's dispute resolution provisions.[85]
- ***Long Phase out of U.S. Tariffs on Imported Japanese Cars and Trucks.*** With up to 30 years before these tariffs are eliminated completely, some experts alleged that the TPP tends to emphasize protection over liberalization.[86] ITAC 2 sees the long phase out period as appropriate to provide Japan with a "sufficient transition period to a more open automotive market."[87]
- ***Slow Liberalization Schedule for Malaysia and Vietnam.*** These countries will complete their vehicle and parts tariff reductions in year 13 year of TPP's implementation, although some of Vietnam's restrictions will remain after full implementation.[88] (Almost all auto

parts from TPP countries will be able to enter the United States duty free as soon as the TPP takes effect, as long as they meet the rules of origin.)

- ***Tracking and Enforcing Complicated Rules of Origin.*** TPP methods permit automakers to import vehicles and parts that contain some non-TPP content (from China or Thailand, for example). While supply chain sourcing is increasingly global, the impact on smaller U.S. parts manufacturers is not clear. ITAC 2 report calls for the U.S. government to monitor and enforce these rules to prevent non-TPP countries from benefiting from the preferential tariff benefits.[89]
- ***Lack of Regulatory Harmonization.*** There are no obligations to require TPP countries to accept motor vehicle imports engineered to U.S. regulatory standards. This means that U.S. producers may need to modify their vehicles before selling them in other TPP member countries. This can be costly, especially in countries where the prospective demand for U.S.-made vehicles is small. ITAC 2 calls the lack of recognition of U.S. standards a "retreat from the longstanding U.S. practice of securing concessions in new agreements that go beyond what had been achieved in prior pacts. As such, this represents a significant missed opportunity."[90]

Services[91]

Background

A major priority for the United States in its negotiations of bilateral and regional FTAs is increased market access for services providers.[92] Congress identified expanded market opportunities in services trade as a principal negotiating objective in the TPA-2015. Cross-border trade in services represents slightly less than one-third of total U.S. trade, and is an area of focus for the United States due to U.S. firms' competitiveness in these sectors. Services accounted for 78% of U.S. private sector gross domestic product (GDP) and 87 million (82%) private sector employees in 2013. [93] The United States consistently runs a surplus in services trade; U.S. services exports surpassed imports by $233 billion in 2014. Some economists argue that the expanded commitments in international services may represent the greatest benefit for the United States in the TPP.[94]

The United States sought to expand on previous commitments the 11 partner countries have made on trade in services, particularly with the five countries with whom the United States does not have existing U.S. FTAs (Brunei, Japan, Malaysia, New Zealand, and Vietnam). For these countries, existing commitments with the United States are based on the multilateral WTO General Agreement on Trade in Services (GATS). Another major U.S. objective was to address new services trade barriers not covered, or covered only partially, in previous trade agreements, and in doing so, potentially influence other ongoing U.S. services trade negotiations, including the Trans-Atlantic Trade and Investment Partnership (T-TIP) with the EU and the plurilateral Trade in Services Agreement (TiSA) on the sidelines of the WTO.[95] Emerging issues in services trade include the prohibition of restrictions on data flows and data localization requirements and treatment of electronic payment card systems.

Unlike tariff barriers, nontariff barriers (NTBs) on services trade that the TPP seeks to reduce and eliminate can take many different forms, making them difficult to quantify and compare across countries. The Organization for Economic Cooperation and Development (OECD) has created indices that provide some measure of services trade restrictiveness.[96] These indices, available for OECD countries and some selected other countries across 18 different services sectors, show considerable variation in services trade restrictiveness among TPP OECD countries (Australia, Canada, Chile, Japan, Mexico, New Zealand, and the United States) and hence the opportunity for liberalization through TPP negotiation efforts. For example, in telecommunications, the index, which takes a value from 0 to 1 (most restrictive), ranges from 0.12 for the United States to 0.30 for Japan and 0.34 for Mexico. Such restrictions are likely even greater among some of the lesser developed TPP countries not included in the OECD database. Similar work by researchers at the World Bank, which covers more countries but in less detail, supports this hypothesis. Their index for overall services trade restrictiveness, which takes a value from 0 to 100, ranges from 11 for New Zealand to 41.5 for Vietnam and 46.1 for Malaysia, although the middle income country of Peru (16.4) scores lower than the United States (17.7).[97]

Due to the complexity of services trade barriers, TPP commitments in several chapters may affect services trade. Chapters with a focus on services-related commitments discussed in more detail below include: Cross Border Trade in Services (Chapter 10), Financial Services (Chapter 11), Temporary Entry (Chapter 12), and Telecommunications (Chapter 13).

EXAMPLES OF TPP SERVICES LIBERALIZATION

A key component of services trade commitments in TPP is liberalization of specific industries. Most U.S. service sectors are already open to international competition and the United States made few commitments that went beyond existing trade agreement obligations. Longstanding restrictions on maritime shipping services, for example, would not be affected by the TPP. Other TPP countries, particularly the five countries without existing U.S. FTAs, opened additional services sectors to U.S. competition. Examples include

- **Japan** would remove preconditions to provide express delivery and insurance services, and allow competing insurance providers access to the distribution network of Japan Post, the Japanese postal provider.
- **Malaysia** would eliminate its foreign capital cap in telecommunications services and all joint venture and performance requirements for 12 service sectors in the upstream oil and gas industry, including drilling services, turbine repair and maintenance, and seismic data acquisition.
- **Vietnam** would remove foreign equity restrictions on freight agency, warehousing, and customs clearance, and eliminate joint venture requirements for freight brokerage and related cargo logistics services.

USITC Estimated Economic Impact

The USITC predicts generally positive results for U.S. services industries from the TPP.[98] The May 2016 study estimates that both services sector output and employment would see increases above a 2032 baseline as a result of the TPP. These gains are small in relative terms (0.1%), but large in absolute terms ($42.3 billion increase in output) given the scale of the U.S. services sector. Both exports and imports are expected to increase above the baseline ($4.8 billion and $7.0 billion, respectively) but the estimated larger growth in imports would lead to an overall decline in net U.S. exports of services. The authors attribute this to a few factors: increased expenditures on tourism abroad (a U.S. services import), due to higher U.S. incomes post TPP; a shift in U.S. productive resources to sectors experiencing greater liberalization in foreign markets, including food and agriculture; and increasing U.S. demand for services imports given output capacity constraints and greater demand for U.S. services exports in TPP countries. The increase in U.S. services exports is estimated to go largely to TPP countries without an existing FTA while the increase in U.S. services imports would come from non-TPP countries, particularly the EU.

Cross-Border Trade in Services

The TPP chapter on cross-border trade in services commits parties to provisions governing situations in which the buyer and seller are located in different territories. As with previous U.S. FTAs, the TPP employs the "negative list approach," that is, the provisions are to apply to all types of services, unless specifically excluded by a partner country in the chapter annex on NCMs. This approach is generally considered more comprehensive than the "positive list approach" used in the GATS, which requires each covered service to be identified. The negative list approach also implies that any new type of service that is developed after the agreement enters into force is automatically covered unless it is specifically excluded. Key provisions include the following:

- nondiscriminatory treatment of services from partner-country providers, including national treatment and MFN treatment;
- no limitations on the number of service suppliers, the total value or volume of services provided, the number of persons employed, or the types of legal entities or joint ventures that a foreign service supplier may employ;
- prohibition on locality requirements that a TPP-based service provider maintain a commercial presence in the country of the buyer;
- support of mutual recognition of professional qualifications for certification of service providers;
- transparency in the development and application of government regulations; and
- allowance for payments and transfers of capital flows that relate to the provision of services, with permissible restrictions in some cases including bankruptcy and criminal offences.

EXAMPLES OF TPP SERVICES NONCONFORMING MEASURES (NCMS)

Each TPP party, including the United States, has a list of specific industries or practices it would exempt from its TPP services trade obligations. Examples include

- **Accounting:** An accountant in **Japan** is required to be qualified as a certified public tax accountant under the Japanese laws and regulations and establish an office within the district of the certified public tax accountant association to which the person belongs.
- **Audiovisual:** In **Vietnam**, the ratio of screening Vietnamese films to total films must be at least 20 percent annually and cinemas should show at least one Vietnamese film between the hours of 18:00 and 22:00.
- **Financial: Malaysia** maintains a "best interest" screening test for granting licenses or approvals for an investment in financial institutions with no specific threshold or established criteria.
- **Hospitality:** To supply food or beverage catering services in **Singapore**, a foreign supplier must incorporate as a limited company, and apply for the food establishment license in its name.
- **Insurance:** In **Australia**, approval of nonresident life insurers is restricted to subsidiaries incorporated under
- Australian law.
- **Legal:** Only **Chilean** and foreign nationals with a residence in Chile, who have completed the totality of their legal studies in the country, are authorized to practice as lawyers, and only lawyers duly qualified to practice law are authorized to plead a case in Chilean courts, or file the first legal action or claim of each party.
- **Maritime:** Only **U.S.-**flag vessels may carry cargo between U.S. ports and must be staffed by U.S. crew.
- **Printing**: Foreign investors in **Mexico** are limited to 49 percent of the ownership interest in a business for printing or publication of daily newspapers written primarily for a Mexican audience and distributed in Mexico.

Express Delivery

The United States made market access of express delivery services a priority in the TPP negotiations, as it has in other recent FTAs, including KORUS. Covered in a chapter annex, the commitments on express delivery focus, in particular, on cases where a government-owned and operated postal system provides express delivery services competing with private sector providers. Japan Post, which also includes banking and insurance services, has been moving towards privatization with an initial public offering of a portion of its shares in 2015, but remains majority owned by the government. Even domestic Japanese competitors in express delivery have argued that the Japanese postal service receives a number of unique advantages. The TPP annex and a separate side letter between the United States and Japan attempt to eliminate those advantages.[99]

TPP, like KORUS, stipulates that the postal system cannot use revenue generated from its monopoly power in providing postal services to cross-subsidize an express delivery service. Vietnam would be exempt from such a rule for 3 years. TPP, however, goes beyond KORUS in its express delivery commitments, and would also require independence between express delivery regulators and providers, prohibit the requirement of providing universal postal service as a prerequisite for express delivery, and prohibit fees on express delivery providers for the purpose of funding other such providers. Unlike KORUS, TPP lacks a specific threshold for the customs *de minimis*, a critical commitment for express delivery providers as shipments valued below the *de minimis* receive expedited customs treatment and pay no duties or taxes. Industry sought a $200 *de minimis*, like that in KORUS, and has noted that TPP parties agreed to periodically review their respective thresholds.[100]

Financial Services

Financial services, including insurance and insurance-related services, banking and related services, as well as auxiliary services of a financial nature, are addressed in a separate chapter as in previous FTAs. The financial services chapter adapts relevant provisions from the foreign investment chapter and the cross-border trade in services chapter. The prudential exception in TPP provides that nothing in the FTA would prevent a party to the agreement from imposing measures to ensure the integrity and stability of the financial system. TPP, like KORUS, distinguishes between financial services traded across borders and those sold by a provider with a commercial presence in the home country of the buyer. In the case of providers with a foreign commercial presence, TPP applies the negative list approach with commitments applying generally except where noted; in the case of cross-border trade, TPP limits coverage to specific banking and insurance services as defined by each country.[101]

Some critics have noted the long list of NCMs. The United States, for example, excludes Government-Sponsored Enterprises such as the Federal National Mortgage Association (Fannie Mae). One of Malaysia's NCMs has received particular scrutiny from the business community, as it would require the Malaysian government's approval for certain bank and insurance investments based on whether such investment is in "the best interest of Malaysia." Services industry representatives have raised concerns over the potential breadth of this exemption given its lack of a threshold or specific definition or criteria.[102]

Financial services are not covered under the e-commerce chapter and therefore not protected by that chapter's new obligations such as the prohibition of localization requirements for data servers and computing facilities. The chapter does, however, have a separate provision prohibiting restrictions on cross-border data flows based on KORUS, which is similar to that found in the e- commerce chapter. U.S. financial services firms and some Members of Congress are concerned about the distinct treatment of the sector because, like many other industries, financial services firms rely on cross-border data flows to ensure data security, create efficiencies and cost savings through economies of scale, and utilize internet cloud services that are often provided by U.S. technology firms.[103] Localization requirements imposed by countries could require companies to have in-country servers and data centers to store data. These types of regulations can create additional costs and may serve as a deterrent for firms seeking to enter new markets or a disguised barrier to trade. Localization supporters, though, claim they increase local control and data security.

In TPP, USTR negotiated for the position advocated by the U.S. Treasury Department and sought flexibility for financial regulators to impose localization requirements. While localization requirements are not currently in place in TPP countries, observers note that Malaysia and Vietnam are considering imposing such regulations. In addition, some stakeholders note concern about other countries, including potential future TPP parties such as South Korea and Indonesia, which have or are considering localization requirements. Treasury Secretary Lew cautioned that options for altering the 12-country agreement are limited[104] and, on May 25, 2016, announced a proposal to resolve the issue in future trade agreements (which would not directly affect TPP commitments).[105]

TPP, like KORUS, also addresses insurance sold by government postal entities. U.S. providers have argued that government-owned and operated insurance providers are not regulated as stringently and, therefore, have a competitive advantage over privately-owned counterparts. TPP would require that parties to the agreement ensure that postal insurance entities are not given advantages over private suppliers, specifically including through regulations, requirements to maintain a license, and access to distribution channels. In some ways, these measures go beyond what was included in KORUS. The separate U.S.-Japan letter on nontariff measures specifically addresses Japan Post's insurance business with clarified and additional commitments by Japan.[106]

For the first time in a U.S. FTA, the TPP also includes commitments on electronic payment card services. The TPP would require that each country in the agreement allow for the supply, by persons of other TPP countries, of electronic payment services for payment card transactions, defined by each country, and generally including credit and debit cards. The provisions on card services would, however, allow for certain preconditions of access, including requiring a representative or office within country.

Temporary Entry for Business Persons

While some services can be traded across borders, services are also traded by a person supplying the service traveling to the location where the service is consumed. This is known as mode 4 delivery in the GATS. TPP, like some previous U.S. FTAs, includes commitments on temporary entry for business persons in order to facilitate such trade. As temporary entry has been a controversial issue in the context of previous trade agreements, the United States did not offer or seek commitments on additional visas for temporary entry, and only agreed to measures on regulatory transparency and predictability. According to the Administration, these rules would not require any change in U.S. immigration laws or regulations, and dispute settlement for this chapter is limited to very specific circumstances.[107] Other TPP parties, however, have made additional access commitments on the temporary entry of business persons, including on length of stay and types of occupations, but these will only apply to the other countries making commitments in this area (i.e., not the United States). Australia, for example, provides categories defining "business visitors" and spells out the conditions and limitations for each category such as "service sellers" who are permitted an initial stay of 6 months up to a maximum of 12 months.[108]

Telecommunications

For the first time in a U.S. FTA, the telecommunications chapter covers mobile service providers. Television or radio broadcast or cable suppliers, though, are not covered. Overall, the chapter applies a market driven approach, enshrining competition and consumer choice in the sector, and promotes the independence of regulators from the regulated. According to the Administration and the industry advisory committee, given current competition in the U.S. mobile market, the United States would not have new obligations resulting from the TPP commitments, but U.S. mobile carriers would gain greater access to markets abroad.[109] The chapter's provisions would require regulatory transparency; that providers can interconnect with one another; that there is reasonable and nondiscriminatory access to networks, infrastructure, government-controlled resources like spectrum bandwidth, for reasonable rates; and protection of the supplier's options for employing technology. The chapter would promote cooperation on charges for international roaming services and allow regulation for mobile roaming service rates. Other provisions aim to ensure that suppliers can resell and unbundle services.

Stakeholder and Industry Views

Services industries generally have reacted positively to the TPP provisions relating to U.S. trade in services, with some key exceptions. The International Trade Advisory Committee for services and finance industries (ITAC 10) reported that the agreement satisfies TPA negotiating objectives and "on balance promotes the economic interest of the United States."[110] Business groups note that for the five countries without existing U.S. FTAs, the provisions in TPP would provide meaningful additional market access.[111] They also highlight new provisions in TPP, particularly those related to data flows and digital trade, as advancing U.S. service firms' interests. Provisions on data flows also affect other (non-services) firms, such as manufacturers who rely on global supply chains and transmitting data across borders. The larger business community also sees additional advances in the TPP, include ensuring electronic payment card services and electronic signatures, as well as addressing mobile telecommunications carriers and international roaming rates.

While business groups generally support the agreement and its impact on services, they have raised some concerns. There has been vocal opposition from some in the services sector, for example, over financial services firms' exclusion from TPP's e-commerce chapter and its provisions prohibiting localization requirements for computing facilities.[112] The U.S. Treasury Department reportedly argued in favor of this exception to maintain regulatory flexibility for requiring local storage of financial firm data; opponents of the provision view it as unnecessary given the general prudential exception in the services chapter.[113] Several Members of Congress have expressed their concerns over this exemption in a letter to USTR, urging the Administration to address the issue both in TPP and in ongoing negotiations.[114] Other issues of concern for services industries include: the long list of nonconforming measures (NCMs) that limit the level of liberalization achieved; what some view as a narrow definition of SOEs, limiting these disciplines' applicability; and the U.S. decision not to negotiate additional commitments on temporary entry for business persons in TPP.[115]

The Communications Workers of America (CWA), a union representing workers in a number of service industries, opposes TPP. They argue that increased access to the U.S. services market and various provisions throughout the agreement, including on government procurement, investment, and data transfers, could have negative impacts on service workers including in jobs such as call centers and data processing.[116] Other groups also oppose TPP, in part, due to certain services provisions, particularly those on financial services. They argue that TPP commitments will restrict the U.S. government's ability to regulate the financial services industry.[117]

Agriculture[118]

Background

Exports make a vital contribution to U.S. agriculture, absorbing about 20% of total agricultural production, while representing a far larger share of the production of certain commodities, including wheat, rice, soybeans, cotton, almonds, pecans, pistachios, and walnuts, to name a few. As such, foreign demand for U.S. food and fiber contributes materially to higher commodity prices and farm income. The positive ripple effects from farm trade extend beyond farmers and ranchers to rural communities to include: farm input industries that provide seed, fertilizer, and machinery; and commodity processors and food manufacturers with a stake in foreign markets. Exports also can contribute to higher input prices for food to the extent that additional foreign demand is not met by an increase in domestic supplies, although commodity costs amount to a fraction of overall retail food prices. Rising farm productivity, market-oriented U.S. farm policies, and the prospect of competing on more favorable terms for a larger share of the faster-growing food markets in many developing countries are among the reasons that negotiations aimed at liberalizing agricultural trade among TPP countries has elicited a high level of interest and broad-based engagement from U.S. agriculture and food industry interests.

It appears the TPP agreement would improve market access for many U.S. food and agricultural products, thus enhancing U.S. competitiveness in a number of markets. At the same time, it also would provide TPP partners with greater access to U.S. markets, thus raising the level of competition from TPP partners.

Three considerations around the TPP are particularly relevant for U.S. food and agriculture. A discussion of these issues and USITC estimates of TPP's economic impact on U.S agriculture is followed by a partial snapshot of some of the higher-profile improvements in market access for agricultural products in the agreement, a summary of selected provisions beyond market access that are of interest to food and agriculture, and a review of industry reactions to the agreement.

Key Considerations

An overarching consideration is that among significant TPP markets, the United States lacks FTAs with five TPP countries—of which the most significant are Japan, Vietnam, and Malaysia. With a combined population of roughly 250 million, these three countries likely offer the greatest potential for boosting U.S. farm and food exports via lower tariffs, or expanded tariff rate quotas (TRQs).[119] Significantly, all three countries impose much higher average applied MFN agricultural tariffs than the United States, which could work to the advantage of U.S. farm and food exports versus domestic suppliers and non-TPP export competitors as tariffs decline under the agreement. [120] In 2014, applied MFN tariffs on agriculture products averaged 5.1% in the United States, 9.3% in Malaysia, 14.3% in Japan and 16.3% in Vietnam.[121] Moreover, existing tariff peaks are far higher for a number of product categories. Examples include dairy and poultry imports into Canada; bovine meat, rice and dairy products into Japan; and Vietnamese tariffs across a number of food categories. Japan is likely the leading agricultural market opportunity in the TPP due to its highly protected farm and food markets, large population, and high per capita gross domestic product. Vietnam, with the fourth largest population in the TPP and a fast growing economy, is generally viewed as a market that could hold significant future growth potential for U.S. farm and food products.

Also significant is that potential key export expansion opportunities for U.S. food and agriculture interests, such as beef and pork to Japan and dairy products to Japan, Canada, and Vietnam, generally are to be phased in over a period of years, if not decades. For certain products in certain countries, including Japan for beef, pork, and whey powder, and the United States for some dairy products, safeguard measures allow for additional tariffs to be imposed if imports should exceed specified thresholds. Generally, the quantitative trigger level for invoking safeguard measures would increase over time, while the duties imposed under the safeguard are scheduled to be reduced or eliminated. At the same time, preferential access that U.S. food and agricultural interests have to markets in Canada and Mexico under the North American Free Trade Agreement (NAFTA) would become available to a wider group of potential competitors over time as tariffs are lowered for TPP countries.

If the United States chooses not to implement the TPP agreement, U.S. agricultural export competitors would have the potential opportunity to gain a competitive edge over U.S. exports of certain products to Japan and elsewhere. This could occur as a result of existing preferential tariff arrangements—such as Australia's FTA with Japan—or by ratifying an agreement similar to TPP without U.S. participation. Also, while the European Union is not party to the TPP, it is negotiating FTAs with Japan, Malaysia, and Vietnam that could enhance its producers' competitive position in those markets.

USITC Estimated Economic Impact

The USITC in its report on TPP of May 2016 concluded the agreement would provide significant benefits to U.S. agriculture.[122] The model estimated TPP outcomes in 2032 for U.S. agriculture compared with a baseline scenario without TPP and reached the following conclusions:

- Agricultural exports would be $7.2 billion higher (2.6%), while imports would increase by $2.7 billion (1.5%). Agricultural output would expand by $10 billion (0.5%), while employment in agriculture also would increase by 0.5%.
- U.S. dairy product exports would increase by $1.85 billion (18%), while processed foods and beef would post gains of $1.54 billion (3.8%) and $876 million (8.4%), respectively. Fresh fruit, vegetables and nuts would see an estimated increase of $575 million (2%), while pork and poultry meat products post increases of $219 million (1.9%) and $174 million (1.3%), respectively. Corn and rice exports are

estimated to be marginally lower with TPP by 0.1% and 0.3%, respectively.

- As for U.S. imports, processed food would increase by $427 million (1.1%), while beef imports would expand by $419 million (5.7%) and dairy products would be $349 million higher (10.3%).
- Export gains stem primarily from greater market access via lower tariffs and expanded TRQs, with the lion's share of the total increase of $7.2 billion concentrated in Japan ($3.6 billion) and Vietnam ($3.3 billion).

Specific Market Access Commitments

A principal negotiating objective for agriculture in the TPA-2015 is to obtain competitive opportunities for U.S. exports of agricultural commodities that are substantially equivalent to those provided to foreign exports in U.S. markets. In part, this is to be achieved by reducing foreign tariffs on U.S. commodities, while providing a reasonable adjustment period for import-sensitive U.S. products. Accordingly, the TPP agreement would affect market access for a broad range of agricultural commodities and food products. What follows is a selection of some of the notable changes included in the agreement. It is not meant to be comprehensive.

- **Beef:** Japan ranks as the largest U.S. export market for beef and beef products, according to the U.S. Department of Agriculture (USDA). Under the TPP agreement, Japan would drop its current tariff on fresh, chilled, and frozen beef from 38.5% to 27.5% in year one, with subsequent annual reductions to 9% by year 16. Japan would lower tariffs on other beef products as well, while Vietnam would eliminate such tariffs, currently as high as 34%, over three to eight years. The United States, for its part, would eliminate tariffs on beef and beef products that range as high as 26.4% in no more than 15 years and in fewer than 10 years in most instances.
- **Pork:** Japan, which also ranks as the leading market for U.S. pork and pork product exports, would immediately cut its tariff of 4.3% on fresh, chilled, and frozen pork cuts to 2.2%, phasing out the residual over nine years. A separate duty on pork cuts under Japan's "gate price system," which acts as a minimum import price, would be lowered immediately to 125 yen per kilogram, from 482 yen now. This duty would then be cut to 70 yen in year five and subsequently lowered each year thereafter to reach 50 yen in year 10. A special

U.S.-specific safeguard would allow Japan to temporarily increase the duty during this transition period if imports were to exceed a trigger level. Vietnam would eliminate tariffs that are as high as 34% on pork and pork products within 10 years, while the United States would immediately eliminate most such tariffs.

- **Poultry:** Canada would allow incremental increases in access to its highly protected poultry and egg markets over five years via new duty-free, TPP-wide TRQs amounting to 2.3% of domestic production for eggs, 2.1% for chicken, 2% for turkey, and 1.5% for broiler hatching eggs. Thereafter, the quotas would be raised moderately each year, plateauing in year 19, at which point these TRQs would amount to 19 million dozen eggs, 26,745 metric tons of chicken, 3,983 tons of turkey and 1.14 million dozen broiler hatching eggs and chicks. Vietnamese tariffs on poultry of up to 40% would be eliminated within 13 years. U.S. tariffs of up to 18.6% *ad valorem* equivalent would be eliminated within 10 years.
- **Dairy:** Opening dairy markets to greater import competition was among the most difficult agricultural issues to resolve during TPP negotiations. Under the agreement, Canada would allow incremental additional access to its highly protected dairy product markets amounting to 3.25% of its output for 2016 under TRQs that would be phased in over five years, with moderate annual increases thereafter. For perspective, this additional access would amount to about 0.3% of current U.S. milk production and would be open to all TPP countries. These Canadian TRQs for dairy products, such as fluid milk, butter, cheese, and yogurt, would increase between 14 and 19 years and then remain fixed. In-quota dairy products would enter Canada duty free. Canada also would eliminate its over-quota tariff of 208% on whey powder over 10 years. Japan would eliminate many tariffs it imposes on cheese imports within 16 years and on whey within 21 years. The United States would gradually phase out tariffs and establish TRQs for dairy products from Australia and New Zealand that would be increased annually. Existing preferential access for Australian dairy products under the U.S.-Australia FTA would be transferred to perpetual TRQs. New U.S. TRQs for Canadian dairy products would be raised gradually each year until year 19, at which point the quantities would remain level.
- **Rice:** Japan, the second-largest overseas market for U.S. rice, would establish a new duty-free quota for U.S. rice of 50,000 tons initially,

rising to 70,000 tons in year 13, but still well below the 165,000 tons the U.S. rice industry had sought. Japan also would allow a broader range of domestic entities to participate in tenders on this additional quota, as well as on 60,000 tons of rice under an existing quota. But Japanese officials indicate that the "minimum mark-up" Japan imposes on rice imports—equivalent to a 15-20% duty according to USA Rice— would continue to be applied to all imports. U.S. tariffs on rice products of up to 11.2% would be eliminated within 15 years.

- **Cotton:** U.S. tariffs on cotton that range up to $0.314 per kg generally would be eliminated by 2022, and in some cases would be removed immediately.
- **Sugar:** Access to the U.S. sugar market would be expanded incrementally by establishing new TRQs for sugar and sugar-containing products totaling 86,300 tons annually, representing 2.4% of U.S. sugar imports in 2014/2015. Australia and Canada would immediately receive new duty-free quotas totaling 65,000 tons and 19,200 tons per year, respectively. The residual would be split between Japan, Malaysia, and Vietnam. The Australian and Canadian TRQs include the potential for expansion in years when additional U.S. sugar imports are required. The additional TRQ for sugar is not expected to threaten the budget neutral requirement of the U.S. sugar program. Japan would provide new TRQs that would expand access to its market for sugar and sweetener-related processed products on a duty-free or preferential-tariff-rate basis, including chewing gum, chocolates and products containing chocolate, confectionery goods and other such products, and would eliminate tariffs on various sweetener products over time.
- **Tobacco:** U.S. tariffs on tobacco of up to 350% would be eliminated within 10 years, while Japan would eliminate tariffs on smoking tobacco and cigars over 11 years, and Malaysia would eliminate all tariffs on tobacco and tobacco products over 16 years. Vietnam would create a TRQ of 500 metric tons for unmanufactured tobacco imports that increases gradually for 20 years with no limit from year 21, while eliminating in-quota tariffs over 11 years and for all tobacco leaf after 20 years. Vietnamese tariffs on blended tobacco, cigars, and other tobacco products would be eliminated over 16 years. A controversy has emerged over a provision in the Exceptions chapter of the agreement that allows countries to deny recourse to protections under the investor-state dispute settlement (ISDS) to tobacco product

manufacturers for claims directed at tobacco control measures. This optional exclusion would not apply to leaf tobacco, although, to the extent that tobacco product sales could be blunted by this provision, it would appear to have the potential to affect sales of leaf tobacco.

Other Agriculture Provisions

The agreement addresses a number of trade-related areas beyond tariffs and TRQs are import to exporters of food and agricultural products, among which are sanitary and phytosanitary measures (SPS), agricultural biotechnology and export programs.

Geographical Indications

Geographic Indications (GIs) are geographical names that act to protect the quality and reputation of a distinctive product originating in a certain region.[123] As such, GIs can be commercially valuable and, as intellectual property, can provide eligibility for relief from acts of infringement or unfair competition. GIs are most often, but not exclusively applied to wines, spirits and agricultural products. Examples of GIs include Parmesan cheese and Parma ham, Champagne, Florida oranges, Idaho potatoes, Washington State apples and Napa Valley wines. GIs have become a point of controversy in international trade because GIs that are considered by some to be protected intellectual property are considered by others to be generic or semi-generic names and thus not protected. For example, "feta" is considered a generic name for a type of cheese in the United States, but is a protected GI in the European Union (EU). As such, U.S.-produced "feta" cannot be sold under that name in the EU. This type of exclusivity can extend beyond the EU, for example, when a third country has agreed to recognize EU-approved GIs under a bilateral trade agreement.

The TPP agreement obligates members that provide for recognition of GIs to make this process available and transparent to interested parties within the TPP, while also providing a process for canceling GI protection. Parties that recognize GIs also are to adopt a procedure by which interested parties may object to the provision of a GI. Among the reasons the agreement lists for opposing a GI are: the GI is likely to cause confusion with a trademark that is recognized within the country, a pre-existing application is pending, or the GI is the customary term for same item in the common language of the country. Specific to wines and spirits that are products of the vine, TPP members are not required to recognize a GI of another member if the GI is identical to the customary name of a grape variety existing in that party's territory. Factors that are relevant in determining whether a term is the customary common name for a good include whether the term is used to identify the good in dictionaries, newspapers and websites, and whether the term is the name by which the good is marketed and referenced in trade in the country.

Finally, with respect to other international agreements involving TPP members that provide for the protection of GIs, the TPP agreement states that members are to make available to interested parties information concerning the GIs involved and to allow them a reasonable opportunity to comment and to oppose the prospective recognition of the GIs. These obligations would not apply to international agreements that were concluded, agreed in principle, ratified, or that had entered into force prior to the entry into force of the TPP agreement.

Sanitary and Phytosanitary (SPS) Measures

As tariff rates have been lowered for food and agricultural products in recent decades, nontariff barriers have gained greater visibility as obstacles to trade. Among the nontariff measures the TPP seeks to address are SPS measures, which consist of actions that address issues of food safety, plant pests and animal diseases.[124] Among SPS commitments the agreement addresses are: the establishment of an SPS committee composed of TPP member representatives; an obligation to base SPS measures either on international standards or on objective scientific evidence and to select risk management measures that are no more trade-distorting than necessary; a commitment to allow for public comment on the development of SPS measures; and the obligation to provide rapid notification of shipments held on importation. Importantly, SPS disputes are to be addressed first in technical consultations among relevant governmental authorities under a procedural timeline established in the agreement. If the issue cannot be resolved through technical consultations, parties may turn to dispute settlement procedures in the agreement.

TPP builds on the WTO's SPS agreement with the introduction of a rapid notification requirement that obligates an importing country to provide notification within 7 days when an inbound shipment is restricted or prohibited. IT also establishes a new rapid response mechanism that allows parties to raise SPS concerns through recourse to Cooperative Technical Consultations by engaging national trade and regulatory agencies with the aim of resolving them within a defined procedural framework and timetable.

Table 3. Tariff Elimination Schedule for Selected Food and Agricultural Products in Selected TPP Countries

Product	Importing Country	Tariff Elimination Timetable
Frozen French fries	Japan	Within 6years
Peanuts and peanut products	United States	Within10 years
Grapes, avocados, strawberries	Japan	Immediate
Fresh/chilled broccoli, tomatoes, lettuce, and garlic	Japan	Immediate
Tree nuts, fresh/dried	Japan	Immediately for most
Tree nuts, fresh/dried	United States	Mostly immediate, but within 5 years
Wine	Japan	Within 11 years

Source: TPP Agreement released November 2015.

Notes: USDA has compiled summaries with additional detail on what the agreement contains in terms of market access for numerous farm commodities groups at http://www.fas.usda.gov/data/tpp-benefits- specific-agricultural-commodities-and-products.

Agricultural Biotechnology[125]

As concerns agricultural products of modern biotechnology, the agreement commits the signatories to increase transparency and provide notification of national laws and regulations of biotech products. It also encourages information sharing on issues related to the occurrence of low-level presence (LLP) of biotech material in food and agricultural products. To minimize LLP occurrences and any disruptions to trade that may result from an LLP incident, both importers and exporters commit to exchange certain information, such as product risk assessments and new plant authorizations.

The agreement also establishes a working group on agricultural biotechnology within the TPP Committee on Agricultural Trade. The working group is to function as a forum for exchanging information on issues such as national laws, regulations and policies affecting trade in biotech products. Finally, the agreement states that parties are under no obligation to adopt or modify existing laws, regulations or policies that apply to biotechnology.

Export Disciplines

On the topic of agricultural export programs, signatories to the agreement commit to eliminate the use of export subsidies, a type of incentive the United States does not employ in any case. The export subsidy ban is seen mainly as setting a standard for future reform on a multilateral basis. A commitment around export credits, credit guarantees, and insurance programs—which the United States does employ—is less ambitious: the agreement merely states the parties will cooperate to develop multilateral disciplines around these programs. The agreement also discourages restrictions on exports of food and agricultural products. To this end, it commits TPP countries to limit such restrictions to six months, and requires a country that imposes such restrictions for more than 12 months to consult with interested TPP importing countries.

Stakeholder and Industry Views

As of the beginning of 2016 numerous interest groups in the food and agricultural sector have passed judgment on the TPP agreement. Supporters include broad agricultural groups such as the American Farm Bureau Federation, as well as specific meat (beef, pork, and chicken) and commodity (wheat, corn, soybean, and peanut) associations. The Grocery Manufacturers Association, representing food, beverage and consumer product companies has also endorsed the agreement. More recently, a number of U.S. dairy groups, including the National Association of Milk Producers, have endorsed the agreement.

The Agricultural Policy Advisory Committee for Trade on the Trans-Pacific Partnership (APAC), which is composed of a broad array of agricultural interests from producer groups to processing and exporting companies, expressed strong support for the agreement, reflecting the views of a "clear majority" of its members.[126] APAC is one of a number of advisory committees charged with assessing whether the agreement promotes the economic interests of the United States and achieves the negotiating objectives that Congress established in TPA-2015.

Support for the TPP agreement, however, is not universal within the food and agriculture sectors. The National Farmers Union (NFU) opposes the deal, contending benefits on the export side of the trade ledger will be overshadowed by greater competition from imports, leading to lower revenues for farmers and ranchers and to job losses. Also opposed to the agreement is the United Food and Commercial Workers Union International (UFCW), which represents workers in the grocery, retail, meat packing and food processing industries. The UFCW faults the agreement for the lack of an enforcement mechanism against currency manipulation, which it contends will nullify the benefits of tariff reductions, while contributing to the transfer of U.S. jobs to lower-wage markets overseas. The NFU and UFCW issued a dissenting minority report as members of APAC.

APAC Representatives of tobacco leaf growers also oppose the agreement. They contend that allowing TPP countries to deny dispute settlement protections to tobacco product manufacturers could have negative ripple effects for U.S. tobacco farmers and could establish a precedent for future trade agreements.

Certain NGOs also oppose the agreement, in part, due to concerns with provisions related to agriculture. These groups argue that the TPP will limit the U.S. government's ability to regulate the country's food supply, raising particular concern with seafood imports from Malaysia and Vietnam. [127] They also take issue with potential food labeling restrictions resulting from TPP commitments, noting that the Congress decided to change its country-of-origin-labeling (COOL) requirements for meat products as a result of a trade dispute with Canada and Mexico in the WTO.

Government Procurement

Background

The Government Procurement chapter sets standards and parameters for government purchases of goods and services among TPP countries. The U.S. trade negotiating objective for government procurement in TPA seeks "transparency in developing guidelines, rules, regulations, and laws for government procurement," but does not address market access goals. The United States is a member of the plurilateral WTO Government Procurement Agreement (GPA) and has sought the inclusion of government procurement provisions in its FTAs. Among TPP partner countries, only Canada, Japan, New Zealand, and Singapore are members of the GPA. All U.S. FTAs—including those with TPP partners Australia, Peru, Chile, Singapore, and NAFTA—include chapters on government procurement. Similar to U.S. obligations in the GPA, although with different schedules of commitments for various government agencies, the FTA obligations provide opportunities for firms of each nation to bid on certain contracts over a set monetary threshold on a reciprocal basis. TPP contains first-ever reciprocal procurement commitments for Vietnam, Malaysia, and Brunei.

Government Procurement Highlights

- First ever reciprocal public procurement commitments from Vietnam, Malaysia, and Brunei.
- Similar to past U.S. FTAs, firms from Vietnam, Malaysia, and Brunei are waived from Buy American restrictions.
- State and sub-federal procurements are largely excluded from TPP.

Supporters of expanded procurement opportunities in FTAs argue that the reciprocal nature of the government procurement provisions in TPP will allow U.S. firms access to major government procurement market opportunities overseas. This market could be quite large. According to the WTO, government procurement typically accounts for 15-20% of a country's GDP, and the size of the government procurement market among GPA members was valued at $1.6 trillion in 2008.[128] In addition, supporters claim open government procurement markets at home allow government entities to accept bids from partner country suppliers, potentially making more efficient use of public funds.

However, others stakeholders contend that public procurement should primarily benefit domestic industries. The Buy American Act of 1933, as amended,[129] limits the ability of foreign companies to bid on procurements of manufactured and construction products. Buy American provisions periodically are also proposed for legislation such as infrastructure projects requiring government purchases of iron, steel, and manufactured products.[130] Such restrictions are waived for companies from countries with which the United States has FTAs or to countries belonging to the GPA.

The United States negotiated only federal procurement, excluding additional state or local procurement commitments in the TPP negotiations. This may be due to resistance among U.S. states to providing access to their procurement markets. States must voluntarily opt in to government procurement commitments in FTAs, but the number of states doing so has dropped substantially from the 37 states that signed up to the GPA to 10 states that acceded to commitments under the most recent U.S. bilateral FTAs with South Korea, Panama, and Colombia.

Key Provisions

In negotiating government procurement agreements, countries set out schedules on: (1) the government entities that will accept bids from overseas companies; (2) the types of procurements that are eligible; (3) monetary thresholds; and (4) exceptions to these commitments. The TPP provides that for eligible procurement opportunities, countries will

- extend national and nondiscriminatory treatment among TPP partners;
- adopt a negative goods coverage schedule (i.e., all goods are eligible unless explicitly excluded, such as defense procurement). Some countries also adopt a negative list for services;
- promote transparency in the tendering process through online tender information and descriptions;
- provide online application and documentation processes without cost to the applicant, and provide for publication of post-award explanations of procurement decisions;
- broaden covered procurement to include public-private partnerships (PPP) and build-operate-transfer (BOT) projects, although Malaysia, Mexico, and Vietnam are excluded from this provision; and
- prohibit offsets.

Countries have made incremental changes in the schedules of covered commitments to provide additional access to TPP partners. Yet, several countries have taken exceptions to their schedules. The United States and four other countries (Malaysia, Mexico, New Zealand, and Vietnam) exclude sub-central (state and local) procurement. Countries that do make sub-national commitments (Australia, Canada, Chile, Japan, and Peru), extend those concessions reciprocally only among themselves.

Thresholds, Transitions and Exemptions. When fully effective, most countries will adopt a baseline threshold of SDR130,000 (about $180,000).[131] However, Brunei, Malaysia, and Vietnam will apply transitional thresholds that shrink over time: 4 years for Brunei, 7 years for Malaysia, and 25 years for Vietnam. Thresholds for sub-federal procurement and construction projects are higher. In addition, Malaysia is allowed to retain its Bumiputera preferences to support the native Malay population, and Malaysia, Mexico, and Vietnam may continue to impose offsets, set-asides and price preferences for varying periods or permanently. For example, Vietnam will be able to set aside 100% of the value of pharmaceutical procurements for the first 3 years, transitioning in installments to 50% in year 16. In addition, Malaysia can exempt any procurements that will "affect Malaysia's essential security interests."

Intellectual Property Rights (IPR)[132]

Background

Intellectual property (IP) is a creation of the mind embodied in physical and digital objects. IPR are legal, private, enforceable rights that governments grant to inventors and artists that generally provide time-limited monopolies to right holders to use, commercialize, and market their creations and to prevent others from doing the same without their permission.

The use of trade policy to advance IPR internationally emerged with NAFTA and the WTO Agreement on Trade-Related Aspects of Intellectual Property Rights (TRIPS). These agreements build on international treaties administered by the World Intellectual Property Organization (WIPO). U.S. trade negotiating objectives in TPA-2015 call for U.S. FTAs to “reflect a standard of protection similar to that found in U.S. law” (“TRIPS- plus”) and to apply existing IPR protection to digital media through adherence to the WIPO “Internet Treaties.” TPA-2015 also includes new objectives to address cybertheft and protect trade secrets and proprietary information.

IP is a source of U.S. comparative advantage, and the Asia-Pacific region is a fast-growing market for U.S. IP-based exports. TPP countries represent more than one-fifth of the approximately $130 billion in IP royalties, license fees, and payments that U.S. exporters received in 2014.[133] According to USITC modeling estimates, improvements in TPP countries’ patent protections to meet TRIPS obligations, led to an 11% or $2.9 billion increase in U.S. IP receipts from these countries in 2010, which could have been even higher with greater levels of patent protection (17% or $5.0 billion higher in 2010).[134]

IPR Highlights in TPP

Provisions on IPR protection and enforcement in TPP that are new or modified compared to KORUS include the following:

Biologics. Requires for biologics a data exclusivity period of eight years or, alternatively, five years coupled with “other measures... to deliver a comparable outcome in the market.”

Digital enforcement. Extends IPR enforcement, including for copyrights, to the digital environment.

Trade secrets. Requires criminal procedures and penalties for trade secret theft, including cybertheft; also clarifies that SOEs are subject to trade secret protection requirements.

Copyright balance. Obligates Parties to "endeavor to achieve an appropriate balance" between users and rights holders in their copyright systems, including digitally, through exceptions for legitimate purposes (e.g., "fair use").

Internet Service Providers (ISPs). Requires "notice and takedown" to address ISP liability while allowing alternative systems to remain for certain countries (e.g., "notice and notice").

Trademarks. Extends trademark protection to "collective marks" and removes administrative requirements to enable easier protection and enforcement of trademarks.

Geographical indications (GIs). Requires administrative procedures for recognizing and opposing GIs, including guidelines for determining when a name is common. Also, for GIs that a Party protects through international agreements, includes requirements on transparency and opportunity to comment or oppose GI recognition. (See "Agriculture" section for more on GIs.)

At the same time, the TPP region poses significant counterfeiting and piracy challenges, including in the digital environment. The USTR continued to designate five TPP parties (among 34 U.S. trading partners) as having IPR regimes of concern to the United States in the 2016 "Special 301" report (pursuant to Sec. 182 of the Trade Act of 1974, as amended). The report reviews the global state of IPR protection and enforcement and designated Chile on the "Priority Watch List" for significant IPR concerns; and Canada, Mexico, Peru, and Vietnam on the "Watch List" for lesser but still notable IPR concerns (see **text box**).[135]

In its FTA negotiations, the United States generally seeks IP commitments that exceed the WTO TRIPS Agreement's minimum standards of IPR protection and enforcement. TRIPS includes provisions on a balance of rights and obligations between protecting private rights holders and securing broader public benefits. Debate persists in U.S. trade policy and more broadly, among developed countries (historically IP generators and exporters) and developing countries (historically IP importers), about this balance.

IPR Protection and Enforcement Issues in TPP Countries

Examples of U.S. IPR concerns with the TPP countries designated in the USTR's *2016 Special 301 Report* include the following.

Priority Watch List

- **Chile:** Need for implementation against unlawful circumvention of technological protection measures (TPMs) and changes to Internet Service Provider (ISP) liability regime to permit effective action against Internet piracy.

Watch List

- **Canada:** Impact of heightened patent utility requirements applied by Canadian courts on U.S. pharmaceutical patents.
- **Mexico:** Limitations in enforcement against transshipment of counterfeit and pirated goods.
- **Peru:** Prevalence of pirated and counterfeit goods, including increasingly online.
- **Vietnam:** IPR enforcement challenges, including lack of resources and lack of deterrence in enforcement actions.

The *2016 Special 301 Report* states that, under TPP, these countries have committed to strengthening their IPR regimes in many of the areas of concern highlighted in the report, as well as other areas. It also states that the United States will work closely with these countries on TPP implementation, which may include bilateral engagement, technical assistance, and trade capacity building.

Source: USTR, *2016 Special 301 Report*, April 2016.

Debate and Stakeholder Views

Among the more controversial aspects of the TPP negotiations were protections for pharmaceuticals through patents and data exclusivity, which raise questions about the balance between supporting innovation and supporting affordable access to medicines. One view is that patents and data exclusivity provide incentives for innovation by enabling right holders to generate profits to recoup R&D and regulatory costs and invest in future innovations. Another view is that patents may raise the costs of drugs and delay the entry of generic competitors into the market, thereby impeding affordable access to medicines. Some observers argue that a narrow focus on patents and data exclusivity masks the other factors that can affect public health, such as the efficiency of health care delivery systems or infrastructure, while others emphasize the significant role of patents and data exclusivity. Such debates have come to a head in terms of TPP's treatment of biologics, a major U.S. innovation sector that can produce life-saving medicines, but for consumers, affordability is a concern both in the United States and abroad.[136]

With copyrights, a longstanding debate concerns the balance between granting copyright holders exclusive rights to control their works and providing certain limitations on that right for "fair use" (e.g., criticism, comment, news reporting, teaching, scholarship, and research). Stakeholders also debate the balance between allowing Internet Service Providers (ISPs) to operate their businesses and providing enforcement procedures to address copyright theft through their networks.

During the negotiations, different stakeholders expressed concern over how TPP's IP chapter compared to other FTAs, chiefly the KORUS and the "May 10th" FTAs, i.e., those then-pending FTAs revised to reflect the May 10, 2007, Bipartisan Trade Understanding (May 10th addressed four different aspects of U.S. FTA provisions, see text box preceding this section for more). Some business groups, especially in the pharmaceutical sector, while broadly supportive of the IPR chapter, express concern that certain aspects of it may be less robust compared to KORUS, while others say that vigilant enforcement of TPP will not lead to any substantive differences from the level in KORUS.[137] Some express concern about the length of transition periods for implementing IPR commitments for certain countries, while others argue that these transition periods reflect TPP countries' development levels and enforcement capacity.

Some groups, particularly those concerned about the impact of strong IP provisions on affordable access to medicines in developing countries, favored maintaining the May 10th approach to patents. Others argued that this approach was specifically tailored to certain FTAs and not intended to be the template for the U.S. approach to patent protections in FTAs going forward. In the end, TPP includes some provisions favorable to both sets of stakeholders, extending some patent and data protections beyond those of the May 10th Agreement, while providing phase-in periods for those new commitments for developing countries.

IP is addressed primarily in a separate chapter in TPP, though other chapters also have some relevance (e.g., investment). The patent section reflects some May 10th elements, but departs in other areas. The IP chapter also contains some new provisions that go beyond existing U.S. FTAs, such as KORUS. IP provisions, including key changes, are discussed below.

Patents

Patents protect new innovations and inventions, such as pharmaceutical products, chemical processes, new business technologies, and computer software. Patent protection in the TPP builds on the TRIPS provisions of the WTO and adapts provisions from previous U.S. FTAs. It broadly seeks to establish consistent and harmonized patent regimes throughout the TPP region. Some of these provisions are specific to pharmaceutical products and are designed, according to recently enacted U.S. trade negotiating objectives, to "encourage innovation and access to medicine."

Patent Subject Matter. TPP reaffirms the familiar language of TRIPS requiring countries to provide a system of patents available for an invention, product or process "if the invention is new, involves an inventive step and is capable of industrial application." In addition to making patents available for "new uses or new methods of using a known product"—the language found in KORUS—TPP also provides for "new processes of a known product."

TPP reaffirms the TRIPS language that a party may exclude from patents diagnostic, therapeutic and surgical methods, and animals other than microorganisms. While it allows parties to exclude plants other than microorganisms from patentability, it does provide for patents for inventions derived from plants.

Access to Medicines. TPP provides that the chapter's obligations "do not and should not prevent a Party from taking measures to protect public health...and, in particular, to promote access to medicines for all." TPP affirms that the chapter should be interpreted as consistent with the WTO Doha Declaration on TRIPS and Public Health (TRIPS Declaration). Parties also may take measures consistent with the TRIPS Declaration in matters regarding protecting test data for pharmaceuticals and biologics.

Patent Term Adjustment. TPP provides that for unreasonable delays (defined as more than five years from the date of filing, or three years from a request for examination) in the patent examination process, applicants may request an extension of the patent term.[138] For pharmaceutical products subject to marketing approval by a regulatory authority, TPP also provides adjustment for a patent term to account for unreasonable delays, although in this case, "unreasonable" is not defined. These provisions follow the KORUS text, but allow Brunei, Malaysia, and Vietnam a five-year transition period. Patent term extension was optional under the May 10th agreement for developing countries.

Protection for Undisclosed Test Data (Data Exclusivity). Often referred to as data exclusivity, this practice provides a period of protection for test data that prevents a generic company from relying on the test data submitted by the originator company in order to gain marketing approval for a generic version of the brand name drug. TPP provides at least five years of data exclusivity for small molecule pharmaceuticals, following the KORUS standard. The May 10th FTAs also provided for five years of data exclusivity; however, they allowed, for countries relying on marketing approval granted in the United States, that period to run concurrently if the country grants marketing approval within six months of receiving an application. The purpose of concurrent period is to encourage the marketing of innovative drugs in developing countries. TPP does not provide for a concurrent exclusivity period. TPP also provides an additional three years of data exclusivity for clinical information supporting a new indication, formulation, or method of administration of an existing approved drug. Under the May 10 agreement, this type of extension was optional. In addition, under TPP, the expiration of the patent cannot limit the period of protection for test data.

Biologics. The issue of data exclusivity for biologics[139] has been especially contentious in TPP. The United States currently provides a 12-year exclusivity period for marketing data submitted with biologics for marketing approval, and sought that standard in the TPP negotiations in line with U.S. negotiating objectives. [140] Other countries have had a range of exclusivity periods, from no period of exclusivity (Brunei) to five years (Australia, Malaysia, New Zealand, Singapore, and Vietnam) to eight years (Japan and Canada). Chile, Mexico, and Peru do not differentiate between data exclusivity for biologics and small-molecule pharmaceuticals, but have 5-year periods for the latter.[141] TPP provides either eight years of data exclusivity, or five years coupled with "other measures" and "recognizing that market circumstances also contribute to effective market protection" to "deliver a comparable outcome in the market." Some Members of Congress have objected to this shortened period of exclusivity, and may seek side letters or other measures to clarify how this provision will be implemented.[142] Australia and New Zealand have indicated that they would not have to make changes to their laws to be compliant with this language.[143] The TPP is the first FTA specifically to include protections for biologics as an obligation.

Patent Linkage. Under this practice, a national regulatory authority (e.g., U.S. Food and Drug Administration) cannot grant marketing approval to a generic version of a drug without the permission of the patent holder. If marketing approval is sought for a generic prior to the expiration of a patent, this patent could delay the access of generic medicines. Previous U.S. FTAs, such as KORUS, mandated the notification of the patent holder and obligated the marketing authority to prevent a generic manufacturer from seeking market approval without the rights holder's consent. TPP continues the notification requirement, but provides more flexibility on the notification system and the procedures (e.g., judicial or administrative proceedings, and remedies, such as preliminary injunctions) for a patent holder to assert his rights, as well as for a party to challenge the patent's validity. While the May 10 agreement required this flexibility only for developing countries, TPP extends it to all countries. U.S. law does not mandate patent linkage for biologics, and this may have been a motivating factor for flexibility concerning patent linkage in the TPP.

Copyright and Related Rights

Copyrights protect artistic and literary works, such as books, music, and movies. The TPP copyright section, broadly speaking, includes copyright protections similar to those in KORUS for literary and artistic works, performances, and phonograms (collectively referred to here as "creative works" and distinguished as needed), and some new features, such as for "fair use" and enforcement.

International Agreements. TPP, like KORUS, requires each party to ratify or accede to several international agreements by the TPP's entry into force. These include the 1996 WIPO "Internet Treaties," which set forth international norms regarding copyright protection in the digital environment.[144] To date, the WIPO Internet Treaties are in force for nine TPP countries, most recently Canada in 2014, although full implementation of the treaties remains a U.S. concern for some countries. Brunei, New Zealand, and Vietnam have yet to ratify or accede to these agreements.

Length of Protection. TPP, like KORUS, increases copyright terms to life plus 70 years, or 70 years from publication for most works. This is higher than the TRIPS Agreement baseline (life plus 50 years). TPP includes phase-in periods for countries currently providing life plus 50 years of protection, which include Brunei, Canada, Japan, Malaysia, New Zealand, and Vietnam.[145]

Exclusive Rights. TPP carries forward KORUS' core copyright protections. Each party must provide right holders the exclusive right to authorize or prohibit the reproduction, communication, and distribution of their works.

Limitations, Exceptions, and "Fair Use." TPP, like KORUS, requires each party to confine limitations or exceptions to copyrights subject to certain conditions. New in TPP is a provision that parties "shall endeavor to achieve an appropriate balance" between users and rights holders in their copyright systems, including digitally, through exceptions for legitimate purposes, such as criticism, comment, news reporting, teaching, scholarship, and research—known as "fair use" in the United States.

Technological Protection Measures (TPMs). TPMs are measures such as encryption to limit unauthorized reproduction, transmission, and use of products. TPP, like KORUS, requires civil, administrative, and criminal penalties for circumventing TPMs or selling devices and services for breaking TPMs, subject to certain exceptions for noninfringing uses. While KORUS appears to confine exceptions and limitations to specified measures, TPP appears to set out broader parameters for providing exceptions and limitations regarding circumventing TPMs. According to USTR, "TPP's anti-circumvention of [TPMs] provisions do not preclude new exceptions, like cellphone unlocking, while still protecting new online services that engage in legitimate digital trade."[146]

Enforcement. The IP chapter's enforcement section includes a number of copyright-related provisions. New provisions in TPP compared to KORUS include extending copyright enforcement commitments to the digital environment and requiring criminal penalties and procedures for camcording in movie theaters. Similar to KORUS is a TPP provision requiring criminalization of the theft of encrypted satellite and cable signals.

Collective Management Societies. TPP includes a new provision that recognizes the importance of collective management societies[147] for copyrights in collecting and distributing royalties based on "fair, efficient, transparency and accountable" practices."

Internet Service Providers (ISPs). ISPs generally are defined as providers of online services for transmitting, routing, or providing connections for digital online communications. Key provisions related to ISPs include:

- ***ISP Liability.*** TPP requires parties to establish or maintain a legal framework and "safe harbors" to allow legitimate ISPs to develop their business while also providing effective enforcement procedures against digital copyright infringement. These include legal incentives for ISPs to cooperate with copyright owners to deter unauthorized storage and transmission of copyrighted materials, as well as limitations in law that preclude monetary relief against ISPs for copyright infringement that, generally speaking, the ISPs do *not* control but that takes place through their systems or networks. KORUS also contains provisions on liability for service providers and limitations.

- ***Notice and Takedown.*** TPP requires parties to adopt "notice and takedown" provisions to address ISP liability, i.e., a requirement for the ISP to remove or disable access to infringing materials on their networks or systems when they receive notice or become aware of the infringement and a liability exemption for an ISP that has taken proper action. It also contains safeguards to protect against abuse of notice and takedown systems. Some find TPP's "notice and takedown" approach similar to that in the U.S. law while others have questioned its consistency. TPP allows certain existing alternative systems for specific countries, such as Canada's "notice and notice" system.

Trademarks

Trademarks protect distinctive commercial names, marks, and symbols. TPP includes provisions on trademark protection and enforcement. Key features are discussed below.

Term of Protection. Under TPP, like KORUS, the term of protection for the initial registration of a trademark and each renewal is no less than 10 years.

Scope of Protection. TPP includes several provisions regarding the scope of trademark protection:

- ***Sound and Scent Marks.*** TPP, like KORUS, extends trademark protections to sounds (stating that marks do *not* have to be "visually perceptible" in order to be registered). Unlike KORUS, TPP does not extend trademark protections to scents, instead requiring "best efforts" to do so. Some stakeholders may value the "best efforts" language as a positive development, but would prefer mandatory protection for scents.
- ***Certification and Collection Marks.*** TPP, like KORUS, extends trademark protections to "certification marks" (e.g., such as the

Underwriters' Laboratory or Good Housekeeping Seal) New in TPP is protection for "collective marks," which is not in KORUS. Certification marks are usually given for "compliance with defined standards," while collective marks are usually defined as "signs which distinguish the geographical origin, material, mode of manufacture or other common characteristics of goods or services of different enterprises using the collective mark."[148]

- ***Well-known Trademarks.*** TPP, like KORUS, extends protection for "well-known marks" to dissimilar goods and services, whether or not registered, so long as the use of the mark would indicate a connection between the goods or services and the owner of the well-known mark and the trademark owner's interests are likely to be damaged by the use. TPP, similar to KORUS, require "appropriate measures" to refuse applications or cancel registrations and prohibit using trademarks that are identical or similar to well-known trademarks for identical or similar goods or services if doing so is likely to cause confusion with the prior well-known trademark.
- ***GI Protection.*** Geographical indications (GIs) protect distinctive products from a certain region, applying primarily to agricultural products (e.g., feta cheese, Parma ham).TPP, like KORUS, requires geographical indications (GIs) to be eligible for protection as trademarks. This provision may be viewed as consistent with the U.S. approach which affords GIs protection through the trademark system. (See Agriculture, above, for more information.)

Exceptions. TPP, like KORUS, allows parties to provide limited exceptions to trademark rights, such as "fair use of descriptive terms," subject to certain conditions.

Trademark System. TPP, like KORUS, includes provisions to enhance efficiency and transparency in parties' trademark systems, such as requiring a system for examining and registering trademarks, the ability to challenge a refusal of a mark, and an electronic system for application and maintenance of trademarks.

TPP expands on KORUS to also prohibit parties from requiring that a mark be recorded as a condition for a trademark owner to be able to pursue certain legal proceedings relating to the acquisition, maintenance, or enforcement of trademarks. The removal of this administrative requirement is intended to enable easier protection and enforcement of trademarks.

Domain Names. Similar to KORUS, TPP requires each party to have a system for managing its country-code top level domains (ccTLDs) and to make available online public access to a database of contact information for domain-name registrants. Going beyond KORUS, TPP requires parties to make available appropriate remedies in which a person registers or holds, with "bad faith intent to profit," a domain name that is identical or confusingly similar to a trademark. This provision is intended to protect against what is often referred to as "cybersquatting."

Trade Secrets

Trade secrets are confidential business information that is commercially valuable because it is secret, including formulas, manufacturing techniques, and customer lists. TPP is the first FTA to require criminal procedures and penalties for trade secret theft, including through cyber means, and including such theft by State Owned Enterprises (SOEs). While some stakeholders view these new commitments on trade secrets as a good first step and a good precedent, others express concern that the provisions lack clarity and do not go far enough.

Industrial Designs

Industrial designs constitute the ornamental or aesthetic aspects of a product. The section on industrial designs is a new provision in TPP. It adds protections beyond the TRIPS Agreement for designs embodied in a part of an article, or a part of an article "in the context of the article as a whole." TPP also contains hortatory language on parties improving their system of design registration.

Investment[149]

Background

The United States, a major source of and destination for foreign direct investment (FDI), negotiates investment rules in its trade agreements to reduce restrictions on investment, protect investors, and advance other U.S. interests. The TPA-2015 includes a principal U.S. trade negotiating objective to reduce or eliminate discriminatory barriers to foreign investment while ensuring that, in the United States, foreign investors are not accorded "greater substantive rights" than domestic investors. The U.S. Model Bilateral Investment Treaty

(BIT) also forms the basis of U.S. investment negotiations and contains "core" protections for investors (see **text box**).

In 2014, TPP countries represented more than 20% of U.S. global FDI (stock and flow), and TPP would cover more FDI than any U.S. FTA (save the potential T-TIP). The United States has bilateral FTAs in force with six TPP countries, all with investment obligations.[150] Still, U.S. investors express concern about investment barriers in the TPP region, including restrictions on investing in certain sectors, discriminatory treatment, and local content requirements.

PROTECTIONS COMMON TO TPP AND U.S. INVESTMENT AGREEMENTS

Market access for investments.

Nondiscriminatory treatment of foreign investors and investments compared to domestic investors and investments (national treatment) and to those of another country (most-favored-nation treatment).

Minimum standard of treatment (MST) in accordance with customary international law, including fair and equitable treatment and full protection and security.

Prompt, adequate, and effective compensation for expropriation, both direct and indirect, recognizing that, except in rare circumstances, nondiscriminatory regulation is not an indirect expropriation.

Timely transfer of funds into and out of the host country without delay using a market rate of exchange.

Limits on performance requirements that, for example, condition approval of an investment on using local content.

Investor-State Dispute Settlement (ISDS) for binding international arbitration of private investors' claims against host country governments for violation of protections in Investment Chapter, along with requirements for transparency of ISDS proceedings.

Exceptions are included, TPP-wide, for essential security interests and prudential reasons, among others.

Debate and Stakeholder Views

Investment negotiations reportedly were among the most difficult in TPP. One issue is the relationship between protecting investors and TPP countries' national sovereignty. Supporters argue that investor protections are central to removing investment barriers and protecting investors from discriminatory treatment. Supporters also argue that U.S. investment agreements do not prevent governments from regulating in the public interest in a nondiscriminatory manner, and that ISDS remedies are limited to monetary penalties and cannot require governments to change their laws or regulations. Critics counter that companies use ISDS to restrict governments' ability to regulate in the public interest (such as for environmental or health reasons), leading to "regulatory chilling" even if an ISDS outcome is not in a company's favor. The United States, to date, has never lost a claim brought against it under ISDS in a U.S. investment agreement. Some opponents express concern that ISDS in TPP could open the United States to more litigation because of the presence in the United States of affiliates of companies from TPP countries like Japan. An ISDS claim brought in 2011 by a Philip Morris subsidiary against Australia under the Australia-Hong Kong BIT challenging its plain packaging requirement for tobacco as an uncompensated expropriation and a violation of minimum standard of treatment (MST) obligations heightened the TPP debate. In December 2015, a tribunal ruled that it lacked jurisdiction to consider the claim.[151] Separately, TransCanada's notice in January 2016 of its intent to challenge the Obama Administration's Keystone XL pipeline decision under NAFTA Chapter 11's ISDS mechanism may further complicate the debate.[152]

Another issue is whether investment rules treat U.S. and foreign investors equally. Supporters stress that ISDS and other protections are reciprocal (i.e., a U.S. investor could use ISDS to resolve a dispute over its investment in a TPP country) and modeled after U.S. law, and, thus, do not afford foreign investors any greater substantive rights than U.S. investors domestically. Critics argue that the use of ISDS implies greater procedural rights by providing foreign investors in the United States with an additional choice of venue.

The fairness and transparency of ISDS procedures have also been a focal point. In general, under U.S. investment agreements, the ISDS tribunal is to be composed of three arbitrators—one appointed by the investor claimant, one by the party, and one by agreement of the disputing sides. Most cases are conducted under rules of the World Bank-affiliated International Centre for Settlement for Investment Disputes (ICSID), or under comparable rules of the United Nations Commission on International Trade Law (UNCITRAL). Both sets of rules include procedures for disqualifying arbitrators for bias.[153] The actual record on ISDS also suggests that tribunal outcomes favor states more often than investors.[154] Critics nevertheless express concern about bias, noting that lawyers can rotate between acting as arbitrators in one case and representing investors in other cases. While transparency in ISDS proceedings has been a common part of U.S. investment agreements, some stakeholders argue that the proceedings are not transparent enough. Limited opportunity for third-parties to express their views in ISDS proceedings also has been an issue.

Also debated is the creation of an appellate mechanism to review ISDS outcomes; such a mechanism is a TPA negotiating objective, but is not included in the TPP. Some argue that this kind of review mechanism could bring some coherence to inconsistent tribunal decisions, resulting in greater certainty about obligations under investment agreements, while others argue that it would lead to additional costs and delays in resolving disputes.

EXAMPLES OF INVESTMENT BARRIERS IN TPP COUNTRIES

Examples of investment barriers identified by USTR in selected TPP countries include:

- **Japan:** Uneven implementation of regulatory reforms to attract FDI, and attitudes toward foreign investors.
- **Malaysia:** Restrictions—such as foreign equity limits and requirements to enter into joint ventures with local firms—in sectors such as retail, telecommunications, financial services, professional services, oil and gas, and mining.
- **Mexico:** In the hydrocarbon sector (opened up to greater private investment by 2013 energy reform legislation), local content requirements and restrictions on using international arbitration to resolve certain investor-state disputes.
- **Peru:** Limits on number of foreign employees in local companies.
- **Vietnam:** Continued land use restrictions for foreigners.

Source: USTR, 2016 National Trade Estimate Report on Foreign Trade Barriers, March 2016.

Other ISDS reforms advanced may affect consideration of TPP. For example, in the T-TIP negotiations, the EU submitted a proposal for a new Investment Court System to replace ISDS; the proposal includes an appellate mechanism.[155] U.S. government officials have questioned the proposal, favoring ISDS to protect investors while balancing other public policy interests. Some businesses argue that it would erode investor protections, while some civil society groups say it does not resolve their concerns. The United States may closely monitor how the EU pursues its new proposal in its other trade negotiations, including with TPP partners. For example, the EU-Vietnam trade agreement includes the main provisions of the EU's proposal,[156] and the EU and Canada have agreed to include the proposal's main elements in the finalized text of their Comprehensive Economic and Trade Agreement (CETA).[157]

Key Provisions

The investment chapter largely reflects the 2012 Model BIT's core investor protections and exceptions (see **text box** above). It also notes that such obligations apply to SOEs. Like other U.S. FTAs, TPP does not have an appellate mechanism. TPP also contains some new provisions that go somewhat beyond KORUS and the model BIT and significantly beyond WTO agreements, which address investment issues in a limited manner. Certain new provisions are highlighted below.

Minimum Standard of Treatment (MST). TPP requires parties to provide MST to investments in accordance with applicable customary international law. New in TPP is clarification that a party's action (or inaction) that may be inconsistent with investor expectations is not, on its own, a breach of the MST, even if loss or damage to the investment follows. Some stakeholders oppose the change as weakening investor protections; they view it as departing from the longstanding approach of linking the MST obligation with an investor's reasonable, investment-backed expectations. Others assert that TPP should clarify that investor expectations remain a criteria that may be considered.[158] Others express concern that the MST obligation is ambiguous and could be used to expand investor protections unduly.[159]

Performance Requirements. Like prior approaches, TPP prohibits parties from imposing specific "performance requirements" in connection with an investment or related to the receipt of an advantage in connection with it. These include prohibitions on performance requirements such as to export a given level or percentage of goods, achieve a given level or percentage of domestic content, or transfer a particular technology. New features of TPP compared to KORUS include prohibitions on performance requirements related to the purchase, use, or according of a preference to a technology of the party (or of a person of the party), and related to certain royalties and license contracts. In addition to addressing concerns in TPP markets, these new features may be geared toward addressing "indigenous innovation" measures such as in China.

Denial of Benefits. TPP's denial of benefits article, among other things, permits a party to deny the investment chapter's benefits to an investor that is an enterprise of another party (and to the investments of that investor) if that enterprise does not have "substantial business activities" in the territory of any party *other* than the party denying benefits, provided that the enterprise is owned or controlled by a person of a nonparty or the denying party. According to USTR, the denial of benefits article allows a party to deny benefits to "shell companies."[160] The article presumably is intended to address some stakeholders' concerns for instance, regarding the ISDS claim filed by Philip Morris (PM) under the Australia-Hong Kong BIT to challenge Australia's plain packaging requirement for tobacco, though PM has stated that its restructuring of PM Australia's ownership to PM Asia in Hong Kong was for legitimate business reasons. KORUS also contains a denial of benefits article, but with some variation.

Government's Right to Regulate. Like KORUS, TPP contains a provision stating that, except in rare circumstances, nondiscriminatory regulatory action by a party to protect legitimate public welfare objectives (e.g., in public health, safety, and the environment) do not constitute indirect expropriation. Debate exists about what exactly are "rare circumstances." New in TPP is a statement that nothing in the Investment Chapter "shall be construed as preventing a government from regulating in a manner sensitive to "health, environmental, and other regulatory objectives," as long as the action taken is otherwise consistent with the chapter. In contrast, KORUS limited the affirmation of a government's right to regulate due to "environmental concerns." USTR contends that the "right to regulate" provision is a stronger safeguard that addresses prior ISDS criticism.[161] Skeptics argue that the new provision does not adequately protect a government's right to regulate because the measures a government may take must be "otherwise consistent" with an Investment Chapter which, from their perspective, has vague provisions (such as for minimum standard of treatment) that can be interpreted in an overly broad manner.[162]

ISDS Proceedings. TPP, like most other U.S. FTAs, includes ISDS. It also contains new provisions on ISDS proceedings, including a:

- requirement that appointments of ISDS arbitrators take into account candidates' expertise or relevant experience with respect to the relevant governing law;

- requirement for parties to establish a code of conduct for arbitrators to provide additional guidance on issues of arbitrator independence, impartiality, and conflict of interest;
- provision allowing tribunals to accept and consider *amicus curiae* (third-party) submissions regarding a matter of fact or law within the scope of the dispute that may assist the tribunal in evaluating submissions and arguments of the disputing parties;[163]
- expanded rules for dismissing "frivolous claims;" and
- clarification that a claimant has the burden of proving all elements of a claim.

Supporters assert that these provisions appropriately balance investor protections and safeguards to protect the public interest.[164] Some, including in the business community, argue that these new provisions weaken investor protections and may delay what can already be a lengthy arbitration process, although other civil society groups argue that the safeguards do not go far enough in protecting the public interest.[165] While some support the clarifying language as reaffirming existing obligations, others express concern that it may be interpreted to change substantive obligations. For example, the clarifying statement on burden of proof potentially could be interpreted to require a different burden of proof for the investor.[166]

Tobacco "Carve-out" from ISDS. TPP gives parties the option to deny ISDS to investors' claims challenging tobacco control measures against manufactured products, for example, relating to the labeling or packaging of tobacco products. Some stakeholders support the carve- out as a way to protect public health interests and to protect tobacco control measures obligated by the World Health Organization's Framework Convention on Tobacco Control from challenge.[167] Others question its need because the investment chapter elsewhere affirms a party's right to regulate to protect legitimate welfare objectives and are concerned about the possible precedent it may set for other products or sectors. Still others, particularly in the tobacco industry, oppose the carve-out as discriminatory against a legally-traded product.[168]

Breach of "Investment Agreement" and ISDS. In addition to permitting an investor to seek ISDS for alleged violations of TPP's core investor protections, TPP also allows an investor to pursue ISDS for a breach of an "investment agreement" (commonly called a "breach of contract") between an investor and a government.[169] At the same time, TPP imposes limits on the use of ISDS to challenge investment agreement breaches, including, broadly speaking, allowing its use only if the investment agreement was signed after TPP's entry into force and the underlying agreement does not include an international arbitration clause. Mexico, Peru, and Canada include additional limitations on the use of ISDS for breaches of investment agreements. For instance, Mexico exempts from ISDS breaches of investment agreements if doing so would be inconsistent with certain sector-specific Mexican laws, such as its hydrocarbon sector.[170]

Financial Services. The Financial Services Chapter provides access to ISDS to resolve certain disputes concerning covered financial services investments. In contrast to prior U.S. FTAs, it allows investors to challenge certain actions by parties for alleged breaches of the MST obligation. Like some other U.S. investment agreements, TPP has a "prudential exception" allowing a party to employ measures for prudential reasons or to ensure the financial system's integrity and stability. The prudential exception in TPP appears to be broader than KORUS because it may be invoked with respect to obligations under the entire agreement except for those in goods and goods-related chapters, whereas the prudential exception in KORUS appears to be restricted to a few select chapters of that agreement (financial services, investment, telecommunications, cross-border trade in services concerning the supply of financial services by an investment). TPP also includes a state-to-state arbitration mechanism constituted under its general dispute settlement provisions that may be used when a party invokes a prudential exception as a defense to an ISDS claim and absent a joint determination by both parties that the regulation is exempt. KORUS also includes a state-to-state arbitration mechanism when a prudential exception is invoked as a defense, but it does not appear to be constituted under KORUS's general dispute settlement provisions.

Exceptions. As with past FTAs, the TPP Investment Chapter has a number of country-specific exemptions. Some of these highlighted by U.S. business groups, include

- ***Foreign Investment Reviews.*** Under TPP, Australia, Canada, Mexico, and New Zealand are exempt from ISDS claims stemming from decisions by these countries under specified laws to reject certain types of investment.
- ***Claims Already Filed in Court or Administrative Tribunal***. TPP exempts Chile, Mexico, Peru, and Vietnam from ISDS claims that investors have already submitted before a court or administrative tribunal in those countries.

These exemptions illustrate the multiple interests with which investor protections may intersect. For example, in terms of claims exemptions, on the one hand, governments may have an interest in reducing duplicative actions. On the other hand, some business groups are concerned that such a prohibition may cause some investors (particularly small investors with limited experience) to lose access to ISDS by raising such issues in local proceedings.

Nonconforming Measures (NCMs). Parties agreed to apply TPP's core investor protections on a "negative-list basis" to all sectors and activities except where they specifically took an exception (known as an NCM). Annex I lists each party's current measures that would otherwise violate the Investment Chapter, but which a party has deemed necessary to maintain. For these, the party agreed to a "standstill," (to not to make the measure more restrictive in the future); and also agreed to a "ratchet" (to use any future liberalization of a measure as the new benchmark for the standstill). TPP includes certain limits (exceptions) on the ratchet mechanism for Vietnam for the first three years after TPP's entry into force under specified conditions. In addition, New Zealand raised the monetary threshold for screening investments from TPP countries and the threshold will increase if New Zealand negotiates higher thresholds in other agreements.[171]

Annex II contains measures and policies on which a party retains full discretion in the future. NCMs vary by party and include restrictions on foreign ownership limitations and operation and on branch numbers, asset requirements, and residency or nationality requirements, for specified investments. On one hand, NCMs may allow parties the flexibility to undertake obligations in a manner sensitive to their needs and interests, while on the other hand, expansive NCMs may limit the extent to which TPP liberalizes investment in TPP countries. In Annex III, Malaysia has also exempted its "best interest to Malaysia" test for approving foreign investment in financial services.

Labor[172]

Background

One of the more controversial issues of the TPP pertains to the scope and depth of provisions on worker rights. Supporters of strong worker rights, such as labor unions and certain nongovernment organizations (NGOs), are concerned that failure to promote and implement these rights, including protection of the right to organize and bargain collectively, could adversely affect wages and working conditions in other countries. This, in turn, could further increase competitive pressures on U.S. workers.

Worker rights provisions in U.S. trade agreements have evolved over time.[173] NAFTA included labor provisions in a side agreement that required all parties to enforce their own labor laws. The side agreement includes a consultation mechanism for addressing labor disputes and a special labor dispute settlement procedure. The enforcement mechanism applies mainly to a party's failure to enforce its own labor laws. Under provisions of the 2002 TPA, seven subsequent FTAs included a similar provision within the main text of the agreement.

More recently, internationally recognized labor principles were included in FTAs with Peru, Colombia, Panama, and South Korea consistent with the May 10th Agreement (see text box above). These four FTAs require parties to adopt and maintain in their statutes and regulations core labor principles of the International Labor Organization (ILO) (ILO Declaration). They also required countries to enforce their labor laws and not to waive or derogate from those laws to attract trade and investment. These provisions are enforceable under the same dispute settlement procedures that apply to other provisions of the FTA, and violations are subject to the same potential trade sanctions. These provisions are continued in the TPP.

ILO Declaration on Fundamental Principles and Rights at Work (1998)

- the freedom of association;
- the effective recognition of the right to collective bargaining;
- the elimination of all forms of compulsory or forced labor;
- the effective abolition of child labor; and
- the elimination of discrimination in respect of employment and occupation.

Labor and civil rights groups have raised concerns about the effects of the TPP on workers. Some labor leaders contend that the TPP's labor provisions are weak and that the agreement would provide incentives for businesses to move U.S. jobs to countries with poor protections for worker rights, such as Brunei, Malaysia, Mexico, and Vietnam.[174] Some Members of Congress are particularly concerned about Vietnam. In order to comply with TPP labor obligations, Vietnam would have to make significant reforms to its labor regime. Some policymakers question whether this is possible. Others are concerned about labor conditions in Brunei, Malaysia, and Mexico and whether these countries would be able to meet TPP labor obligations.[175] Proponents of the agreement contend that the TPP would help these countries build their capacity to support labor protections, enhance economic growth, and support thousands of high-paying U.S. jobs, particularly in the high tech and electronics sectors.[176] The Obama Administration asserts that the TPP includes the strongest labor standards of any existing U.S. FTA and that it would allow the United States to "write the rules of the road in the 21st century," especially in the Asia-Pacific region.[177]

Key Provisions

TPP labor provisions are in the main text of the agreement and subject to the same dispute settlement mechanism, including potential trade "sanctions," that applies to other chapters of the TPP. TPP parties agreed:

- to adopt and maintain laws and practices consistent with the ILO Declaration (see box above);
- to adopt and maintain laws and practices governing acceptable conditions of work with respect to minimum wages, hours of work, and occupational safety and health;
- not to waive or derogate from labor laws and practices mentioned above in a manner affecting trade or investment; and
- not to fail to effectively enforce their labor laws through a sustained or recurring course of action or action in a manner affecting trade or investment.

For the first time in a U.S. FTA, the parties also agreed to protect against degradation of fundamental worker rights or working conditions in export processing zones. If a party believes that another TPP country is not meeting its labor commitments, the agreement establishes a means for the public to raise concerns with TPP governments. The agreement also provides for transparency and access to fair and equitable administrative and judicial proceedings, as well as for a mechanism for cooperation and coordination on labor issues, including opportunities for stakeholder input in identifying areas of cooperation.

In addition, and new to the TPP, the United States negotiated separate labor consistency agreements with Vietnam, Malaysia, and Brunei, countries of particular concern for the United States in terms of labor protections. The consistency plans commit Vietnam, Malaysia, and Brunei to undertake specific legal reforms and implement other measures related to freedom of association and collective bargaining, forced labor, child labor, employment discrimination, acceptable conditions of work, institutional reforms and capacity building, transparency and sharing of information, and a review mechanism for implementation of the plan. Most of the commitments must take place before the TPP can enter into force with these countries.

All three plans are subject to labor consultations under the Labor Chapter and to the dispute settlement provisions of the TPP agreement. A previous labor consistency plan was negotiated with Colombia in conjunction with the U.S.-Colombia FTA, but it was not part of the FTA itself, nor subject to the dispute settlement provisions of that agreement. In addition, the United States can suspend additional tariff reductions on Vietnamese products five years after entry-into-force on a U.S. determination that Vietnam has not implemented the plan's provision on the establishment of grassroots labor unions.

Environment

Background

Like the chapter on worker rights, the scope and depth of the TPP's environmental provisions are the subject of ongoing debate.[178] Supporters of environmental provisions seek to ensure minimum standards of environmental protection in partner countries to stem a perceived "race to the bottom," in which countries reduce protection or do not enforce existing standards to attract trade or investment. Supporters of strong environmental provisions in FTAs also note that while many of the provisions in the environmental chapter are covered by multilateral environmental agreements (MEAs), those agreements do not have effective enforcement mechanisms, whereas FTAs contain a dispute settlement mechanism that could result in penalties (i.e., withdrawal of trade concessions).

Other stakeholders, however, contend that environmental provisions are not germane to, and should not be included in FTAs. Several countries in the TPP negotiations reportedly sought weaker disciplines, and sought to remove those commitments from being subject to dispute settlement.[179] Others claim that the enforcement of environmental provisions in existing FTAs is lacking. They point to continued disputes over illegal logging in Peru, despite commitments to protect against such acts in the U.S.-Peru FTA.

As with the U.S. position on worker rights, environmental provisions in U.S. FTAs have evolved over time. Environmental provisions were originally placed in side-letters in the NAFTA agreement containing "enforce your own laws" provisions and a special consultation mechanism and dispute settlement procedure. Under TPA provisions of the 2002 Trade Act, seven subsequent FTAs included a similar enforce your own laws provision within the main text of the agreement. The May 10th Agreement provisions (see text box in appendix) added an affirmative obligation for FTA partner countries to adhere to multilateral environmental agreements (MEAs) and allowed for environmental disputes under the FTAs to access the full dispute settlement provisions of the agreements. These provisions generally were followed in the TPA-2015. The TPP environmental chapter reflects some aspects of recent U.S. FTAs, differs in some aspects, and addresses additional topics not previously considered.

Key Provisions

The chapter obligates each party:

- not to fail to effectively enforce its environmental laws through a sustained or recurring course of action or inaction to attract trade and investment;
- not to waive or derogate from such laws in a manner that weakens or reduces the protections afforded in those law to encourage trade or investment; and
- to ensure that its environmental laws and policies provide for and encourage high levels of protection, and also strive to improve its levels of environmental protection.

The agreement also:

- recognizes the sovereign right of each party to establish its own levels of domestic environmental protection, its own regulatory priorities, and to adopt or modify its priorities accordingly;
- acknowledges a party's right to exercise discretion with regard to enforcement resources; and
- provides for the resolution of disputes; a party may seek recourse to the dispute settlement mechanism of the agreement, following the exhaustion of consultations.

Recent U.S. FTAs have required the parties to "adopt, maintain, and implement" seven enumerated MEAs.[180] TPP requires parties to affirm their commitment to implement the multilateral environmental agreements to which they are a party. However, TPP only requires the "adopt, maintain, and implement" language with regard to CITES (see below), but variously addresses protections contained in other MEAs. Parties "shall maintain" measures consistent with the Montreal Protocol, which is referenced by footnote.

To comply with the MARPOL agreement, each party "shall take measures" to prevent the protection of the marine environment from ships and maintains statutes in compliance with MARPOL, also referenced by footnote. The other MEAs are not referenced, but some provisions address the subject matter of those accords. One reason for this difference in treatment of the MEAs may be that all TPP parties are not signatories to each of the 7 accords.

Fisheries and Fishing Subsidies. For the first time in an FTA, the TPP contains measures to combat overfishing and unsustainable utilization of fisheries, combats illegal, unreported and unregulated (IUU) fishing activities, and promotes conservation of marine mammals. Negotiations to restrict fishing subsidies occurred as part of the WTO Doha Round, but agreement remained elusive. The TPP requires the countries "to seek to operate" a fishing management system to prevent overfishing and overcapacity, reduce by-catch of nontarget species and juveniles, and promote the recovery of overfished stocks. It also prohibits specific[181] subsidies that negatively affect stocks in an over-fished condition and prohibits subsidies to vessels engaged in IUU fishing. Subsidies negatively affecting fish stocks must be brought into conformity within three years, although Vietnam may request a two-year extension while it completes its stock assessment. TPP parties shall "promote the long term conservation of sharks, marine turtles, seabirds, and marine mammals." While measures concerning sharks "should include, as appropriate," collection of species data, fisheries by-catch mitigation, and finning prohibitions, these provisions have not been interpreted as not actually banning shark finning.

Conservation. As noted above, TPP commits the parties to adopt, maintain, and implement laws and regulations to achieve compliance with the CITES treaty. The parties commit to combat the illegal take and trade in wild flora and fauna, including to prevent the trade of wild flora and fauna in violation of the laws of other countries. While TPP does not implement the Ramsar Convention protecting wetlands, it "commits" the parties to take measures to protect "specially protected natural areas, for example, wetlands."

The chapter mentions illegal logging in the context of "exchanging information and practices" for protecting wild flora and fauna, and promoting government capacity for sustainable forest management.

The parties also recognize the importance of cooperative measures—while not making any affirmative commitments—pertaining to trade and biodiversity, invasive alien species, transition to a low emissions economy, and the promotion of environmental goods and services.

E-Commerce, Data Flows, and Digital Trade[182]

Background

The volume of data transmitted across borders is growing (**Figure 7**). With 43.4% of the world's population online today, cross- border data flows have increased 45 times since 2005.[183] Digital trade includes not only end-products such as movies or video games, but also the means or "lifeblood" of the rest of the economy, enhancing productivity and overall competitiveness of an economy. Examples include transmitting information a manufacturer needs to manage global value chains, communication channels such as email and Voice over Internet Protocol (VoIP), and financial services used in e-commerce or electronic trading.

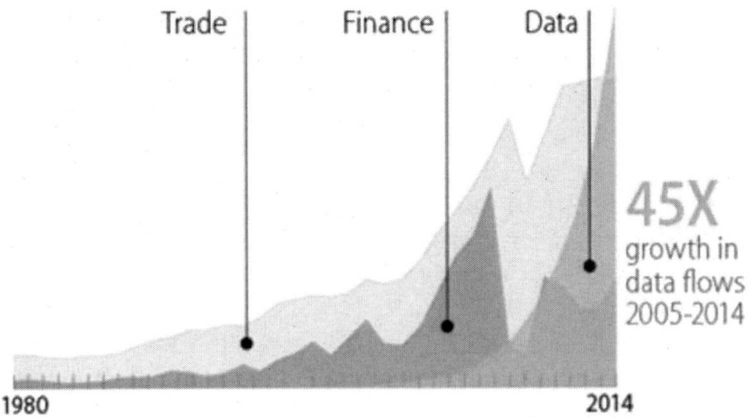

Source: McKinsey Global Institute, Digital Globalization: The New Era of Global Flows, March 2016.

Figure 7. Growth in Global Data Flows.

In 2014, the United States exported $399.7 billion in digitally-deliverable services, and imported $240.8 billion, creating a surplus of $158.9 billion. Digitally-delivered services were half of all U.S. services imports and 56% of services exports.[184] Furthermore, the United States is the largest producer of digital content that Internet users consume worldwide.

Congress established principal negotiating objectives in TPA-2015 on digital trade in goods and services, as well as on cross-border data flows. The objectives include equal treatment of electronically delivered goods and services, as compared to physical products, protection of cross-border data flows, and prevention of data localization regulations, as well as duties on electronic transmissions. The Industry Trade Advisory Council on Information and Communication Technologies Services and Electronic Commerce (ITAC 8), in its report to USTR, endorsed the TPP, finding that the agreement meets the objectives, promotes the economic interests of the United States, and provides equity and reciprocity for the sectors represented by the ITAC.[185] While most industry stakeholders support the digital trade provisions as breaking new ground in this emerging area,[186] some have raised concerns over certain exceptions, particularly the exclusion of financial services from the data localization provisions (see Financial Services section).[187] Other stakeholder groups have argued that the provisions go too far and may limit a government's flexibility to adopt strict privacy laws.[188]

Key Provisions

The electronic commerce chapter broadly covers all industries but explicitly excludes government procurement and financial services, which each have separate chapters. Overall, the chapter aims to promote digital trade and the free flow of information, and to ensure an open internet. While the majority of the obligations related to digital trade are found in the E-commerce chapter, there are relevant provisions in other chapters, including the Financial Services, IPR, Technical Barriers to Trade, and Telecommunications.

Some of the innovations in TPP on digital trade include provisions to:

- prohibit cross-border data flows restrictions and data localization requirements, except for financial services and government procurement;
- prohibit requirements for source code disclosure or transfer as a condition for market access, with exceptions;

- require parties to have online consumer protection and anti-spam laws, and a legal framework on privacy;
- prohibit requiring technology transfer or access to proprietary information for products using cryptography;
- clarify IPR enforcement rules to provide criminal penalties for trade secret cybertheft;
- encourage cooperation between parties on e-commerce to assist Small and Medium-Sized Enterprises (SMEs), and on privacy and consumer protection;
- promote cooperation on cybersecurity;
- safeguard cross-border electronic card payment services; and
- cover mobile service providers and promotes cooperation for international roaming charges.

State-Owned Enterprises

Background

U.S. government and business stakeholders have raised concerns over competition with companies linked to the state through ownership or influence. As a result, they supported new specific TPP disciplines to address such competition. According to analysis by the OECD, state- owned enterprises (SOEs), which traditionally have focused primarily on domestic markets, increasingly compete with international private sector actors.[189] Governments may provide these state-owned or -supported businesses with preferential treatment—such as subsidies, low cost credit, preferential access to government procurement, and a different regulatory environment—compared to private sector competitors, thereby distorting competition and market access. Such advantages may also be directed toward companies not owned but significantly favored or supported by a government. In the context of the TPP, the SOE presence in Vietnam, which accounted for over 40% of all Vietnamese enterprise pre-tax profits in 2013, has been a particular focus, although Malaysia and Singapore also have important SOE sectors.[190] In addition, as the TPP could become a template for a larger Asia-Pacific FTA or future WTO negotiations, wider applicability of these provisions to SOEs in other countries, particularly China, may be envisioned.

In TPA-2015, Congress supported new rules and disciplines on SOEs in U.S. trade agreements as a principal negotiating objective. It directs the Administration to eliminate or prevent unfair trade advantages by state-owned or state-controlled enterprises and to ensure they act on the basis of commercial considerations.

Reaction to the SOE provisions in TPP is mixed. Most groups argue that these disciplines represent a positive first step in establishing international commitments on SOEs and their competition with private firms.[191] Given the potential impact of these provisions on a range of industries, several private sector Industry Trade Advisory Committees (ITAC) generally express support for the SOE commitments. Many of these reports, however, also acknowledge that there are a number of exceptions to these disciplines (nonconforming measures), including all sub- federal SOE activity, and they express concern about the effectiveness and enforceability of the commitments in practice.[192] Other observers are more critical of the provisions, viewing their broad exemptions as a negative precedent. These analysts take particular issue with what they view as a limited definition of SOEs in the agreement, and argue that TPP negotiators should have directly restricted the presence of SOEs in certain sectors rather than attempt to address their potential harm to private sector actors.[193]

Key Provisions

Chapter 17 of the TPP includes the most substantive disciplines on SOEs of any U.S. FTA. NAFTA and subsequent U.S. FTAs with Australia, Chile, Colombia, Peru, and South Korea have minimal disciplines on what they term "state enterprises." Though the specific details vary among these agreements, they are generally limited to two commitments: nondiscriminatory treatment in the sale of goods or services by state enterprises, and clarification that other commitments in the agreement also apply to such enterprises, whenever the state delegates some type of regulatory or administrative authority to the state enterprise. The U.S.-Singapore FTA includes somewhat more extensive provisions on SOEs.[194] Related multilateral commitments under the WTO include Article XVII of the General Agreement on Tariffs and Trade (GATT 1994), but this provision focuses narrowly on state-trading enterprises, entities understood to have some influence on the exports and imports of a particular good.

The provisions in TPP go beyond these existing commitments to address potential commercial disadvantages to private sector firms from state-supported foreign competitors receiving preferential treatment. Like previous U.S. FTAs, most TPP provisions on SOEs also apply to designated monopolies. TPP also includes an agreement to conduct further negotiations on SOEs after 5 years with the intent to reduce nonconforming measures, and extend SOE disciplines to cover competition in the services sector in a non-TPP market. Key provisions include:

- **SOE Definition.** Refers to an enterprise principally engaged in commercial activities if the government owns more than 50% of capital share, controls more than 50% of voting rights, or selects a majority of board members.
- **Delegated Authority**. Would require, like previous U.S. FTAs, that SOEs and designated monopolies adhere to all provisions of the agreement when governments delegate to them regulatory or administrative authority.
- **Nondiscriminatory Treatment/Commercial Considerations**. Would require SOEs and designated monopolies of a party to make their purchase and sale decisions based on commercial considerations and in a nondiscriminatory manner with respect to goods and services bought or sold by other TPP country firms.[195]
- **Noncommercial Assistance/Adverse Effects/Injury.** Would prohibit noncommercial assistance (i.e., funds, loans, or goods and services at more favorable rates than commercially available) provided by or to SOEs, if it adversely affects the interests of other TPP parties or causes injury to another TPP country's domestic industry. Domestic supply of services by SOEs would generally be excluded from these provisions.
- **Transparency.** Would require each TPP country to provide a list of all SOEs within six months of entry into force. Also would require countries to respond to requests for information regarding ownership, revenue, and management of SOEs and noncommercial assistance received. Brunei, Malaysia, and Vietnam are generally exempt from the chapter's transparency commitments for five years, though certain country-specific transparency commitments would apply.
- **Exceptions.** Generally excluded from these provisions are: SOEs with revenue below a certain threshold that adjusts for price level changes in three year intervals (starting at 200 million SDR generally and 500 million SDR for Brunei, Malaysia, and Vietnam for 5 years);[196] a party's supply of goods and services for its own government functions; sub-central SOEs and designated monopolies for nearly all commitments; government actions in economic emergencies; government procurement; sovereign wealth funds; pension funds; and

trade and investment financing provided it is not intended to displace commercially available financing or offered on terms more favorable than available through the market. In addition to these general exclusions there are a number of country- specific exemptions to some or all of the disciplines. Many of these exclusions relate to SOEs owned by sovereign wealth funds, as well as those dealing with natural resources, development financing, including housing finance, and national broadcasting associations. Most countries have also exempted government actions to support indigenous peoples.

EXAMPLES OF SOE NONCONFORMING MEASURES

- **Canada**—would exempt noncommercial assistance to the Canadian Dairy Commission regarding the sales, production, and cross-border trade of dairy products;
- **Chile**—would retain ability for its national television station to provide preferential treatment to Chilean content and receive noncommercial assistance;
- **Malaysia**—would exempt all Malaysian SOEs from commitments affecting preferential purchase arrangements benefitting bumiputera, SMEs, or certain regions, but all Malaysia's SOE exemptions cannot account for more than 40% of an SOE's budget for purchase of goods and services;
- **Mexico**—would retain ability for the national petroleum company to make purchases on a preferential basis from national firms in its exploration and production activities;
- **United States**—would exempt the Federal National Mortgage Association, Federal Home Loan Mortgage Corporation, and the Government National Mortgage Association from nondiscriminatory treatment obligations, allowing them to restrict certain loan repayment guarantees to loans by U.S. enterprises; and
- **Vietnam**—would exempt all Vietnamese SOEs from obligations regarding nondiscriminatory treatment in their purchasing activities, allowing them to accord preferential treatment to Vietnamese SMEs.

Currency[197]

Background

For some Members of Congress, a key issue in the TPP debate has been how to combat the "unfair" exchange rate policies of other countries. Some Members of Congress and policy experts argue that U.S. companies and jobs have been adversely affected by the exchange rate policies adopted by China, Japan, and a number of other countries. They allege that these countries use policies to "manipulate" the value of their currency in order to gain an unfair trade advantage against other countries, including the United States. Given the impact exchange rate values can have on trade flows, some Members have advocated that currency manipulation be addressed in trade agreements, including the TPP.

Other Members and policy experts have questioned whether currency manipulation is a significant problem, how it can be measured, and whether it can be addressed effectively in trade agreements. They raise questions about whether government policies have long-term effects on exchange rates, whether it is possible to differentiate between "manipulation" and legitimate central bank activities, and the net effect of currency manipulation on the U.S. economy. They have also raised concerns that more aggressive measures to combat currency manipulation could lead to a tariff war or put restrictions on U.S. monetary policy.

The June TPA-2015 included, for the first time, a principal negotiating objective addressing currency manipulation, calling on negotiators to seek related provisions. The principal negotiating objective outlined a number of possible remedies to prevent and combat unfair currency practices, including enforceable rules, transparency, reporting, monitoring, and cooperative mechanisms.

Joint Declaration

Largely in response to the TPA-2015, monetary authorities from the 12 TPP countries initiated negotiations and in November 2015 released a declaration to address unfair currency practices. [198] While the declaration was released concurrently with the text of the TPP, it is a separate agreement from the TPP. The declaration has three major parts:

- **Commitment to Avoid Manipulation.** Reaffirms IMF commitments to avoid manipulating exchange rates to gain an unfair competitive advantage, and commits countries to pursue exchange rate policies that reflect underlying economic fundamentals, avoid persistent exchange rate misalignments, and refrain from competitive devaluations and exchange rate targeting for competitive purposes.

- **Transparency and Reporting.** Requires public release of relevant data, including interventions in foreign exchange markets and foreign reserve holdings, as well as IMF's annual assessment of their exchange rate.
- **Multilateral Dialogue.** Establishes a group of TPP macroeconomic officials, with possible IMF participation, to meet at least annually to discuss macroeconomic and exchange rate policy issues, including transparency or reporting, and policy responses to address imbalances.

The joint declaration would take effect when TPP enters into force and would apply to countries that accede to the TPP in the future, subject to additional transparency or other conditions determined by the existing TPP countries. The Treasury Department emphasizes that this declaration, for the first time in the context of a free trade agreement, addresses unfair currency practices by promoting transparency and accountability. However, the declaration does not include any enforcement mechanism on currency manipulation, the inclusion of which some Members advocated.

Nontariff Barriers

Technical Barriers to Trade

Background

Technical barriers to trade (TBT) are standards and regulations that are intended ostensibly to protect the health and safety of consumers or other legitimate purposes, but through design or implementation, may discriminate against imports. In order to minimize trade distortion, WTO members must adhere to the Agreement on Technical Barriers to Trade. The WTO TBT Agreement and subsequent U.S. FTA TBT chapters cover voluntary standards that industries apply, technical regulations that governments impose for health and safety purposes, and assessment procedures that governments employ to determine that a product meets required standards. FTA provisions establish rules and procedures for member countries to follow, including making sure that standards, technical regulations, and conforming assessment procedures are applied without discrimination and in a manner not more trade restrictive than necessary. It addition, they require that members practice transparency as regulations are developed and applied, that international standards are used where appropriate, and that the domestic technical regulations of trading partners are recognized as equivalent to domestic regulations when possible. A key provision of the WTO TBT Agreement is that members have a central point of inquiry from which firms can ask for information on standards and regulations.

Key Provisions

The TPP builds on the TBT agreement and prior U.S. FTAs in several ways. It would:

- provide opportunities for partner countries to comment on proposed standards and regulations and the implementation of regulations;
- require nondiscriminatory treatment for conformity assessment bodies, including nongovernmental bodies;
- extend transparency obligations to include placing new TBT proposals and rules on a single website, broadening the range of TBT measures notified to the WTO;
- allow interested stakeholders from others parties to participate in the development of technical regulations, standards, and conformity assessment procedures by central government bodies, and adopt U.S. style notice and comment periods;
- mandate a "reasonable interval"—generally defined as no less than 6 months— between adoption and implementation of new standards, as well as business compliance with new standards;
- establish a Committee on Technical Barriers to Trade to promote and monitor the implementation and administration of the agreement and strengthen cooperation.

The TBT chapter includes seven sectoral annexes: wine and distilled spirits, pharmaceuticals, medical devices, cosmetics, proprietary formulas for prepackaged food and food additives, information and communications technology products, and organic products. These include sector-specific obligations aimed at reducing unnecessary barriers to trade in these products.

Regulatory Coherence

With average tariffs already low in many countries throughout the Asia-Pacific, nontariff barriers, including inefficient and unpredictable regulatory processes, can be a significant impediment to market access for U.S. goods and services exports. While nontariff and regulatory barriers are addressed in provisions throughout the agreement, the TPP includes a new stand-alone chapter specifically on regulatory coherence. The goal of this new chapter, according to the USTR, is to ensure a regulatory environment throughout the Asia-Pacific that includes hallmarks of the U.S. regulatory system, such as transparency, impartiality, due process, and coordination across government, while affirming the rights of TPP countries to regulate their economies to promote legitimate public policy objectives.[199] To achieve these dual goals the chapter focuses on recognized best practices and good governance frameworks, rather than proscribing specific regulatory actions or outcomes.

The regulatory coherence chapter recommends that TPP partner countries "endeavor" to establish domestic regulatory structures similar to the U.S. Office of Information and Regulatory Affairs in the Office of Management and Budget, a venue to vet proposed regulations and their compliance with domestic law and policy, as well as with trade agreements and other international obligations. Aside from seeking to assure regulatory consistency among various domestic agencies, TPP countries would also be encouraged to conduct regulatory impact assessments that would assess the need for a given regulation, conduct cost-benefit analysis, and assess alternatives to the proposed regulation, as well as seek to assure transparency and openness in the rule-making process. TPP would establish a regulatory coherence committee among TPP members to review implementation of the chapter's commitments and consider future priorities related to regulatory coherence. In addition, TPP would encourage cooperation among the countries on regulatory coherence activities, and would require notification to the committee of steps taken to implement the chapter.

While the agreement establishes new commitments related to regulatory process, the commitments appear largely to require self-enforcement among the 12 countries. Each TPP party would make its own determination of what regulations are covered under the agreement. Nothing in the chapter is subject to TPP's dispute settlement mechanism.

Transparency and Pricing of Health Care Technology and Pharmaceuticals Annex

The debate over access to medicines encompasses other issues beyond pharmaceutical patent protections. Several TPP negotiating partners administer a national formulary for medicines purchased by the government for their national health services.[200] These formularies often rely on generic drugs to the extent possible to maintain availability and contain costs. The U.S. pharmaceutical industry has expressed concern that the practices and procedures in national healthcare programs, including New Zealand's Pharmaceutical Management Agency (PHARMAC), which maintains the New Zealand formulary, put "innovative pharmaceutical products," often made in the United States, at a disadvantage. They contend that access to the country's health care technology markets can be blocked by government's use of nontransparent procedures that do not provide due process.[201] The annex on "Transparency and Procedural Fairness for Pharmaceutical Products and Medical Devices" (Annex 26-A) is located in the chapter on Transparency and Anti-corruption (Chapter 26). As its name suggests, it is dedicated to promoting transparent and fair procedures to parties, concerning the listing of new pharmaceutical products or medical devices for reimbursement purposes. The key provision of the annex requires countries to make available to an applicant either (1) an independent review procedure, or (2) an internal review process, to reconsider a determination not to list a pharmaceutical or medical device for reimbursement. The addition of an internal review process differentiates the TPP from KORUS, which required the establishment of an independent review process. In addition, the parties agreed to consider reimbursement funding in a specified time frame. The annex does not apply to government procurement of pharmaceuticals or medicals, nor does it "modify a Party's system of health care in any other respect." The provisions are not subject either to state-to-state or investor-state dispute settlement.

Customs and Trade Facilitation

Background

Customs valuation and trade facilitation have been long-standing, if unheralded, provisions in U.S. FTAs that aim to ease and expedite the passage of goods over borders through streamlined, transparent, and more accountable customs procedures, and reduce associated transaction costs. OECD research has shown that addressing these issues, which provide the basic framework for how goods move from country to country, can reduce overall trade costs by 10-15%, with the greatest reduction in costs in lower income countries.[202] Because of the potential benefits to the global trading system, improvements in customs and logistical procedures have figured prominently in WTO negotiations and form the core of the 2013 WTO Trade Facilitation Agreement (TFA). Such provisions have taken on new significance as global supply chains have increased the number of times intermediate goods cross borders and, hence, the cost of customs bottlenecks to the world economy.

Industry stakeholders generally support the commitments achieved on customs and trade facilitation in the TPP. On the whole, the Industry Trade Advisory Committee on Customs Issues (ITAC 14) found the agreement "fair and balanced" with similar but expanded provisions to recent agreements.[203] ITAC 14 and other advisory committees, including those representing the services industries, have expressed concerns over the lack of a fixed *de minimis* threshold for customs duties given the importance of this provision in streamlining trade. They note that the parties have agreed to review this issue periodically and encourage the U.S. government to pursue a commercially relevant value.

Key Provisions

The TPP chapter on customs and trade facilitation would generally seek to ensure an efficient, timely, and transparent customs process, with relevant information readily available and easily accessible to businesses.[204] Issues addressed include publication and sharing among TPP parties of customs information, the release of goods and issuance of advance rulings by customs authorities, treatment of express delivery shipments, nature of penalties for violation of customs laws, and risk management techniques for targeting inspection efforts on high-risk shipments. Given the magnitude and frequency of U.S. trade with TPP partners, changes in customs procedures could have a significant impact on companies engaged in trade throughout the region. Some commitments in TPP are similar to those in previous U.S. trade agreements and are already in force between the United States and its current FTA partners.

On some customs issues, the TPP has more extensive commitments than previous FTAs. In other aspects, TPP commitments are less stringent. Generally, the TPP would go beyond the commitments included in the WTO TFA. Differences with existing agreements include:

- **Automation.** A new provision would encourage creation of a single-access window whereby importers and exporters can electronically complete any requirements in one entry point.
- **Advance Rulings.** TPP would require advance rulings to be issued within 150 days of receipt by the customs authority, an increase over the 90 days allowed in the KORUS FTA. There is no deadline in the WTO TFA.
- **Advice/Information.** A new provision would require parties to provide an expeditious response to requests for information regarding issues such as quotas, country of origin markings, and eligibility requirements for repaired and altered goods.
- **Express Shipments.** TPP would require special customs procedures for express shipments, including release within six hours, and a *de minimis* threshold—no specific amount is required—below which goods are not subject to customs duties. The KORUS FTA required release within four hours for express shipment and fixed the *de minimis* threshold at $200 or more.
- **Penalties.** A new provision would place parameters on penalties imposed by a customs administration that go beyond previous U.S. FTAs. Such penalties may be imposed only to the person legally responsible for the breach of law, must be commensurate with the degree and severity of the breach, must be accompanied by an explanation in writing, and proceedings must be initiated within a fixed and finite time period.
- **Release of Goods**. TPP would require general release of goods no longer than the time required to comply with laws and within 48 hours of arrival, where possible. New provisions would provide some protections to importers when customs authorities release goods while holding some type of financial collateral.

Other Provisions

Competition Policies

National competition laws and regulations are intended to protect consumers by ensuring that one firm does not so dominate a sector of the economy as to inhibit market entry and stifle competition. Some U.S. FTAs have included provisions to limit the trade-distorting effects of such laws. Among other things, U.S. FTAs require that the United States and the partner country(ies) inform persons from a partner country, who may be subject to administrative actions under domestic antitrust laws, of related hearings and provide them the opportunity to make their case. Under these FTAs, the partner countries agree to cooperate in enforcing competition laws through the exchange of information and consultation.

The TPP includes commitments on competition policy similar to previous U.S. FTAs, including that such commitments are not subject to dispute settlement. Previously, the limited U.S. FTA commitments on SOEs and designated monopolies were included in the competition policy chapter. In TPP, these issues are addressed in a separate and more extensive chapter (see "State- Owned Enterprises"). TPP includes some commitments that go beyond the recent KORUS FTA. These include provisions related to: protection of confidential business information, private rights of action in pursuing enforcement of national competition laws, and laws protecting consumers from fraudulent or deceptive commercial practices. In addition to the general carve out from dispute settlement, the competition provisions largely will not apply to Brunei until after either 10 years or its establishment of a national competition authority and laws.

Transparency and Anti-Corruption

Transparency. Like the commitments on regulatory coherence, the TPP provisions on transparency relate to the broader governance framework within which each TPP party will administer its laws, rules, and regulations that may affect TPP commitments. These provisions largely follow those included in previous U.S. FTAs, including KORUS. Such provisions would require the publication of all TPP-relevant measures a country may take, with time allowed for comments before such measures take effect. TPP would require countries to "endeavor to publish" proposed regulations no less than 60 days prior to the date on which comments are due, whereas KORUS requires that parties "should in most cases" publish not less than 40 days before comments are due. The agreement would also require due process with respect to administrative proceedings, including a review and appeal of such determinations.

Anti-Corruption. TPP also includes commitments that would require measures to fight corruption, a number of which are not included in the KORUS FTA. Like KORUS, the TPP would require laws or measures making corruption and bribery criminal offenses, substantive penalties for such offenses, and protections for parties that report bribery. TPP includes additional commitments, not found in KORUS, such as requiring monetary sanctions for bribery offences and disallowing the deduction of those sanctions from tax liabilities, prohibiting specific corrupt acts relating to financial reporting and accounting standards, and requiring that no party fail to effectively enforce its anti-corruption commitments as a means to encourage trade and investment, subject to discretion on domestic allocation of resources. TPP also includes language that would require parties to endeavor to adopt a number of measures to prevent corruption among public officials and the private sector such as training, transparency, and disciplinary actions. The agreement would also require Japan to ratify the *U.N. Convention against Corruption* (UNCAC). As of December 1, 2015, Japan is the only TPP country that has not yet ratified UNCAC.[205]

Dispute settlement applies both to the transparency and anti-corruption commitments with some limitations with respect to enforcement of anti-corruption laws. Additional commitments related to transparency and procedural fairness for pharmaceuticals and medical devices are included in an annex to this chapter. For more on these commitments, see "Transparency and Pricing of Health Care Technology and Pharmaceuticals."

In its chapter on transparency, the KORUS FTA also includes a provision that prohibits the United States and South Korea from discouraging their residents' purchase of goods and services from one another. A similar clause is not found in TPP.

Trade Remedies

Trade remedies are measures designed to provide relief to domestic industries that have been injured or threatened with injury by imports. They are regarded by many in Congress as an important trade policy tool to mitigate the adverse effects of unfairly traded imports and import surges on U.S. industries and workers.

The three most commonly used trade remedies are: (1) *antidumping* (AD) remedies, which are designed to provide relief from the adverse price effects of imports sold at less than fair-market value; (2) *countervailing duty* (CVD) remedies, which are used to counter the adverse effects on domestic industry of foreign government subsidies that lower the cost of imports; and (3) *safeguard* actions, which are employed to permit temporary relief so that domestic industries can adjust to the adverse effects of surges in fairly-traded imports. These actions are sanctioned by the WTO as long as they are undertaken in a nondiscriminatory and transparent manner and are consistent with rules specified in WTO agreements.

Congress has repeatedly insisted, including most recently through the TPA-2015, that the United States retain the right to use trade remedies to counter unfair trade practices and import surges and rigorously enforce its trade laws. This objective is reflected in existing U.S. FTAs.

TPP would preserve each party's rights and obligations under the General Agreement on Tariffs and Trade (GATT) regarding global safeguard and AD/CVD measures, as previous U.S. trade agreements have done. TPP includes additional provisions on transparency and due process in pursuing AD/CVD remedies. With regard to safeguard actions, TPP, like previous U.S. FTAs, also describes the precise terms of their use in the context of injury due to increased imports under the agreement, including guidelines on addressing import injury from multiple parties. Following an investigation and affirmative determination of injury by relevant domestic authorities, TPP would allow for a withdrawal of trade concessions for affected products (i.e., returning duties to their pre-agreement levels). The agreement also stipulates certain standards regarding safeguard measures such as their duration (generally no more than two years) and would require notification among the TPP parties of any safeguard actions. If one party implements a safeguard measure, TPP would provide that other affected parties be afforded additional liberalization or may suspend tariff concessions of an equivalent nature.

Development and Capacity Building

A notable aspect of the TPP is the variation among partners in terms of economic development. TPP does not have a distinct set of provisions applicable only to developed or developing countries. Some of the countries, however, particularly Brunei, Malaysia, and Vietnam, have longer phase-in periods before several of their commitments take full effect, and many have extensive nonconforming measures excluding certain sectors, industries, and practices from various TPP provisions.

The agreement includes two related chapters (development, and cooperation and capacity building) addressing issues dealing with this variation in economic status among the countries. Neither chapter is subject to dispute settlement and the commitments in both are largely hortatory, with the exception of establishing committees to exchange information and discuss further possible actions. The chapter on development would require TPP countries to recognize the importance of broad-based economic growth, consider activities to help women take advantage of the agreement, and encourage developing skills in science and technology. The chapter on cooperation and capacity building would require the TPP countries to establish a contact person for coordination on capacity building, and would commit the countries to work to provide the resources necessary to implement the agreement.

As in previous trade agreements, the TPP would not commit the United States to a particular level of funding for trade capacity building (TCB). The U.S. government, however, provides ongoing assistance to a number of FTA partners relating to implementation of trade agreement commitments. For example, a 2008-2011 U.S. Agency for International Development (USAID) project provided $6.2 million to support efforts by the Dominican Republic to implement the DR- CAFTA, including assistance related to customs, SPS, environmental standards, labor standards, and other provisions. TCB is a major component of U.S. foreign assistance—the United States committed $594 million to TCB in FY2014, with major categories including trade-related agriculture ($109.5 million), competition policy, business environment and governance ($69.4 million), trade-related labor ($56.9 million), and customs operations ($54.3 million).[206]

Small- and Medium-Sized Enterprises

Small- and medium-sized enterprises (firms with less than 500 employees by the U.S. definition, or SMEs) account for the majority of firms involved in international trade (about 97%), but they account for a relatively small share of the value of direct U.S. trade (about 30%). In fact, in 2013, eight firms alone accounted for more than 10% of all U.S. exports and imports.[207] SMEs, however, also participate in trade indirectly as suppliers, providing parts and components into the supply chain of larger, finished products that can be exported. That contribution may not always be reflected in U.S. trade data. Though SMEs represent a relatively small share of U.S. trade by value, they employ approximately half of the U.S. workforce in the nonfarm private sector.[208] In addition, academic studies have shown that small businesses are important for job growth, but this appears to be due more to their age than their size—small firms are typically also young firms—suggesting policies aimed at job growth may be better targeted toward young firms than small firms.[209]

The characteristics of SMEs and their relatively small presence in U.S. trade have led to government efforts to improve SME access to international markets. The USTR commissioned a series of reports from the USITC regarding the role of SMEs in U.S. exporting activities.[210] Those reports identified barriers limiting SME access to foreign markets, and surveyed SMEs for suggestions on policy changes that could ease SME exporting activities. An increased focus on FTAs and other trade agreements was among the top three most frequent responses provided.[211]

Seeking to enhance SME engagement in international trade, the TPP negotiators agreed to a stand-alone SME chapter. Although this goes beyond previous U.S. FTAs, the chapter includes few commitments. Disciplines would require TPP countries to make the agreement and some analysis of its SME-relevant provisions available on a website. In addition, TPP would establish a committee to consider further efforts to assist SMEs in trade matters. Nothing in the chapter would be subject to the agreement's dispute settlement mechanism. Negotiators originally described SME's ability to engage in trade as a "cross-cutting" issue in the TPP, noting that disciplines throughout the agreement could impact SMEs. For example, new provisions on digital trade could be salient for SMEs in allowing them to reach new markets. While stakeholders generally support the transparency measures in TPP for SMEs, some have argued that negotiators missed an opportunity to facilitate trade for SMEs by failing to establish a fixed *de minimis* threshold on customs shipments, the value beneath which imports receive expedited and duty-free customs treatment.[212] They argue this would have been particularly beneficial for SMEs as a way to minimize burdensome customs procedures for small-value shipments.

INSTITUTIONAL ISSUES

The TPP contains provisions related to dispute settlement and governance of the agreement. Given that the TPP is viewed as a "living agreement," it contains procedures for the accession of new members, the negotiation of new provisions, and the creation of a Free Trade Commission to oversee the agreement.

Secretariat

Generally, U.S. FTAs have minimal structures; they do not have free-standing secretariats and TPP is no exception. From NAFTA onward, they have included a commission co-chaired by USTR and trade ministers of the respective parties to the agreement. In keeping with this practice, the TPP provides for the establishment of a Free Trade Commission (Commission). The Commission is tasked with: (1) supervising the implementation and operation of the agreement; (2) considering any proposals to amend or modify the agreement; (3) supervising work of committees established under the agreement; and (4) seeking to resolve disputes arising from its interpretation or application (also see dispute settlement, below). Examples of modifications could, for example, be agreements to accelerate tariff elimination, modify rules of origin, or amend the list of covered goods and services in the government procurement chapter. The Commission would meet within one year of the entry into force of the agreement and periodically as the parties decide thereafter. All decisions would be taken by consensus. Any changes to the agreement made by the Commission that require changes to U.S. law would need congressional approval.

Dispute Settlement (DS)

The TPP, as well as previous U.S. FTAs, provide options to resolve disputes arising under the agreement. These are in addition to procedures with regard to investor-state dispute resolution (discussed above). In general, TPP is designed to resolve disputes in a cooperative manner. A party first seeks redress of a grievance through a request for consultation with the other party. These steps include:

- initial consultations between the parties;
- good offices, conciliation, or mediation; and (if no resolution); and
- establishment of a dispute settlement panel.

Panels would be composed of three arbiters, of whom each side appoints one and the third is appointed by mutual consent. Failing that, the third is selected from a list of individuals who are not nationals of either side. After the panel makes its decision, the unsuccessful party would be expected to remedy the measure or practice under dispute. If it does not, compensation, suspension of benefits, or fines have been traditional remedies. In cases in which a dispute is common to both WTO and FTA rules, a party can choose the forum in which to bring the dispute, but cannot bring the dispute to multiple fora. Although State-State dispute settlement use has been infrequent under U.S. FTAs, the size of the potential TPP, the inclusion of new members, and the negotiation of new provisions may cause increased utilization of the dispute settlement forum among the parties.

The applicability of DS for certain provisions was an issue in the negotiations. For example, the labor consistency plans for Vietnam, Malaysia, and Brunei are subject to DS, whereas Colombia's separate labor action plan was not subject to DS. As noted above, the applicability of DS to the environmental provisions was a subject of contention in the negotiations. Some provisions not subject to dispute settlement include:

- the regulatory coherence chapter;
- the competition chapter;
- the SME, development, and cooperation and capacity building chapters;
- certain commitments by Malaysia in the SOE chapter for two years after entry into force; and
- the Annex on pharmaceutical and medical device reimbursement.

A "Living Agreement"

The TPP is envisaged as a "living agreement," one that is open to new members willing to sign up to its commitments and to addressing new issues as they evolve. The TPP provides that countries can amend the agreement by consensus, through consideration by the TPP Commission. Such an amendment, however, could only take effect after each party's legal process is completed. Any amendment requiring changes to U.S. law would need passage of implementing legislation to take effect.

The TPP provides for accession by "any State or separate customs territory that is a member of APEC," or other state by consensus of the parties, that is prepared to meet the standards of the agreement. Following a request to join addressed to the depository of the agreement (New Zealand), the TPP Commission would establish a working group to negotiate the proposed terms and conditions. All parties must agree to the terms and conditions negotiated by the working group through their domestic ratification process. For the United States, that would mean the introduction and passage of implementing legislation by Congress.

While the expansion of the TPP's membership beyond Asia-Pacific countries has been contemplated, as a trans-Pacific agreement, to date, it has focused on APEC countries. Of these, there are many potential candidates, from relatively advanced economies such as South Korea and Taiwan, to middle-income states with dynamic economies and youthful populations like

Thailand or the Philippines. Other countries beyond APEC, such as Colombia and Costa Rica, have expressed interest, and it is conceivable that additional countries or trade blocs beyond the Pacific shores could link up to the agreement in the future. Policymakers in TPP countries have ventured that China may seek to join at some point, provided that it could adhere to the standards of the agreement.

The accession process raises the question of whether a country, especially one with political or economic heft, can be expected simply to join an agreement already negotiated or whether it would or should have input on the existing agreement, especially if the goal is to produce a free trade area for the Asia-Pacific, or beyond. Yet, reopening the agreement's substantive provisions with each new entrant—as opposed to its market access provisions which presumably would need to be negotiated with each existing member regardless—offers up its own difficulties. The WTO accession process, whereby countries agree to the established WTO rules, but negotiate on market access, could serve as a template.

Relationship to Existing Agreements

Each party to the TPP previously has concluded FTAs with multiple TPP members. This circumstance has raised the issue of the relationship of the TPP to previous agreements. Article 1.2 of TPP declares the intention of the parties for it to "coexist" with their international agreements, and in a situation of inconsistency, for the relevant parties to work toward a mutually agreeable solution. The *Vienna Convention on the Law of Treaties* also provides guidance on the interpretation of precedence between agreements:

> When all the parties to the earlier treaty are parties also to the later treaty but the earlier treaty is not terminated or suspended in operation .... the earlier treaty applies only to the extent that its provisions are compatible with those of the later treaty. (Article 30.3)

This provision can be interpreted to mean that the latter treaty applies when there is a conflict, but that an earlier provision could apply in situations where the subject matter of a provision of the earlier treaty is not addressed in the later agreement. In cases where the market access provisions differ between a previous agreement and a later one, it could be up to the exporter as to whether to seek the benefits under the old agreement or the new. Given that the new agreement is likely to achieve further liberalization, the new agreement would most likely be used by the exporter. However, in some cases, such as the phased elimination of tariffs or cases of more favorable ROO, exporters may continue to invoke the provisions of the old agreement, at least until the transition periods of the new agreement are completed.

ISSUES FOR CONGRESS

Congress has taken a strong interest in the TPP since the negotiations were launched in 2008. Hearings have been held, and many Members have expressed views on the negotiations through letters and consultations with the Administration and with stakeholder groups. Congress may consider the agreement from several perspectives if it considers implementing legislation.

Comprehensive, High-Standard Agreement

As the largest FTA negotiated by the United States, the TPP brings together a large and expanding group of countries representing various levels of development. Likewise, with 30 chapters in the agreement, it is the most comprehensive FTA in terms of breadth of commitments undertaken by the United States. On one hand, the TPP would incorporate provisions on new trade barriers, such as digital trade and additional intellectual property rights. On the other hand, certain aspects of the agreement differ from previous U.S. FTAs, and are considered by some stakeholders as less ambitious. For example, the agreement includes the longest U.S. tariff phase-out (30 years) ever in an FTA and excludes more agricultural product lines from complete liberalization than many previous FTAs. Some industry stakeholders have raised concerns over such issues as: less than 12 years of data exclusivity for biologic drugs, as found in U.S. law; the exclusion of tobacco control measures from the ISDS procedures of the investment chapter, unlike any prior FTA; the exclusion of financial services from disciplines on data localization, one of the TPP's innovative provisions; and the more flexible rules of origin for autos and auto parts than those prescribed in NAFTA, among other issues. Meanwhile, some NGO stakeholders were disappointed in certain provisions in the environmental chapter, as compared with previous U.S. FTAs. The negotiators and other stakeholders, however, would argue that these provisions were the result of compromise in order to achieve a final agreement among such a diverse membership.

Key questions for Congress include:

- Did the United States achieve its objective of creating a "comprehensive, high- standard" agreement, including in comparison with previous FTAs and commitments in the WTO?
- Has the TPP set the appropriate framework and precedent for future trade negotiations, particularly on new issues?

Role and Timing of TPA and Negotiating Objectives

TPA-2015 sets forth U.S. negotiating objectives for future U.S. trade agreements as a condition for their expedited legislative consideration, and provides a method to remove expedited treatment if an agreement does not make sufficient progress toward those goals. TPA objectives include traditional goals such as reducing barriers to various types of trade (e.g., goods, services, agriculture, electronic commerce); protecting foreign investment and intellectual property rights; encouraging transparency, fair regulatory practices, and anti-corruption measures; ensuring that countries protect the environment and worker rights; providing for an effective dispute settlement process; and protecting the U.S. right to enforce its trade remedy laws. They also include goals reflecting recent developments and emerging issues, such as objectives on state-owned enterprises, regulatory coherence, trade in the digital environment, and trade in green technologies. In practice, negotiating objectives are written to be flexible enough to allow the Administration to negotiate agreements with other countries, as well as keep current with an evolving international trading system. This flexibility, however, leaves open to interpretation what constitutes "progress in achieving the purposes, policies, priorities, and objectives" of TPA: the standard an agreement must meet in order for its implementing legislation to receive expedited congressional consideration.

Key questions for Congress include:

- Does the TPP make progress in achieving the trade negotiating objectives of TPA?
- Under what circumstances could the expedited procedures of TPA be removed for TPP?

Potential Economic Impact

The current debate over the TPP and its potential impact on the U.S. economy is one component of a larger national conversation on employment opportunities, income and wealth distribution, and the general economic well-being of the U.S. middle class. Economic theory and empirical evidence during the post-war period support the lowering of international trade barriers as a tool for economic growth as a result of increased efficiency, productivity, cost savings, and consumer choice due to greater competition. At the same time, increased trade can lead to job loss and economic dislocation in importing-competing sectors. Jobs with expanding firms may require new skills or relocation, potentially making it difficult for dislocated workers to find new employment.

Estimates of the economic impact of the TPP will likely form an important part of the congressional debate. Deriving these estimates, however, is a difficult and imprecise task. Beyond changes in tariffs and quotas, which form only a portion of the TPP commitments, economic modeling efforts are limited by difficulties in accurately measuring existing trade barriers and their potential changes. In addition, the choice of modeling techniques and assumptions necessary to generate estimates can alter outcomes. Already a number of studies on the TPP have been released, some with very different conclusions. In May, the USITC released the official USG nonpartisan and objective analysis of the agreement's potential economic impact, estimating a small positive benefit to the U.S. economy from the TPP. Key questions for Congress include:

- Do U.S. worker dislocation and retraining programs provide adequate adjustment support for workers disadvantaged by trade, including the retraining and relocation assistance that may be necessary to find alternate employment in competitive industries?
- Do U.S. workers have the skills needed to take advantage of opportunities in a globalized world? If not, who should provide those skills?
- What criteria should be used to evaluate the reliability of the various estimates of TPP's economic impact?

The TPP and U.S. Trade Policy

The U.S. pursuit of the TPP and the outcome of the negotiations raise questions regarding its possible impact on the status and shape of current and future U.S. trade policy. With the Doha Round in abeyance, the United States has turned to the negotiation of 'mega-regional' FTAs such as the TPP and T-TIP as alternative venues for negotiating trade liberalization. These negotiations offer some advantages, namely the potential for deeper liberalization than that achievable through the consensus-based multilateral trading system. These agreements also have the potential to guide and encourage further liberalization through other venues both multilateral and regional. However, as with previous FTAs, the TPP may create trade diversion (i.e., trade patterns that reflect preferential tariff treatment rather than comparative advantage), undermining the broader economic goals of U.S. trade policy. In addition, they could create a two tier global economy, where the rules of the multilateral trading system are different from these mega-regional agreements and potentially impeding trade between the two tiers.

Key questions for Congress include:

- Does the TPP signal the beginning of the end of WTO trade negotiations or could it serve as a building block for a more viable multilateral trade system through the WTO that responds to trade challenges of the 21st century?
- What impact will the TPP have on the WTO as an institution, including on some of its most effective functions, such as the resolution of international trade disputes?

Strategic Considerations

Supporters also frame the TPP in terms of its potential strategic value for the United States, relating to U.S. influence in geo-political and economic spheres in the Asia-Pacific region. China is not a signatory to the TPP agreement, but, in some ways, the debate over the accord includes China. During a time when China's rise and North Korea's growing nuclear and missile capabilities are testing the U.S.-based status quo, TPP proponents argue that the TPP is part of a broad foreign policy strategy to promote greater respect for, and ensure a primary U.S. role in establishing, the next generation of international trade rules and norms in the Asia-Pacific region. The Administration has touted the importance of writing these rules, warning that if the United States does not, China will. The implication is that the rules and disciplines China would seek to impose would be less robust and, perhaps, would be counter to U.S. economic and geo-political interests.

Key questions for Congress include:

- How do the potential strategic effects of the TPP compare to its economic value, and how should one weigh such considerations in an overall assessment of the agreement?
- Are U.S. and Chinese visions of international trading norms fundamentally different or do initiatives by both regional powers advance the same underlying goals?

Potential Consequences of Not Ratifying the TPP

Some analysts have asserted that failure to pass the TPP could have significant implications for the United States both economically and strategically. Given the recent flurry of concluded or implemented trade agreements between major U.S. trading partners (e.g., Australia-Japan, China-South Korea, EU-Vietnam), and the progress in the RCEP negotiations, it is clear that the regional and international trade architecture will continue to evolve with or without U.S. participation. Economically, this means that without the TPP, U.S. goods and services could be at a further disadvantage in foreign markets in which other countries, but not the United States, have negotiated trade agreements. Strategically, they argue that ratification of the TPP may be tied to perceptions of U.S. credibility as a negotiating partner and that countries could interpret a failure of TPP in the United States as a symbol of the United States' declining interest in the region and its inability to assert leadership.

Key questions for Congress include:

- What would be the impact on U.S. trade policy and perceptions of U.S. leadership in the Asia-Pacific region if the TPP is rejected by Congress or is delayed indefinitely?
- How will congressional consideration of TPP affect U.S. credibility in future bilateral, regional, and international trade negotiations?

Implementation, Future Expansion, and Institutional Issues

Congress may look forward as it debates the TPP, considering issues relating to the agreement's potential implementation and expansion. FTA implementing legislation typically requires that the Administration certify the partner countries are prepared to meet their obligations before an agreement can enter into force for the United States. A number of commitments, however, will continue to be phased in over time. Some Members have questioned the commitment of future administrations to ensure that TPP provisions are adequately and equally enforced. Specific issues have been raised with regards to the implementation of IPR commitments, labor and environment provisions, and the removal of nontariff barriers, among other matters. Congress may also consider the institutional structure of the TPP agreement—potentially the largest U.S. FTA— including the congressional role in any expansion of TPP, both in terms of members and content. The accession of new members likely would require implementing legislation, thus requiring congressional approval, if only to amend the U.S. tariff code and impose requisite rules of origin. Implementing legislation would also be required for changes to the agreement that would alter U.S. law. While TPA requires congressional notification for beginning trade negotiations, Congress may also consider whether to require prior congressional approval to negotiate with potential new participants due to the expandable nature of the TPP.

- Has the United States adequately funded implementation and enforcement efforts for past FTAs? How should the U.S. government ensure that TPP commitments are fully implemented, and subsequently enforced?
- What factors should be considered in assessing the suitability of a country for membership? Would amendments or changes to the agreement not requiring changes to U.S. law be subject to congressional approval?

CONCLUSION

The potential Trans-Pacific Partnership agreement has both economic and broader strategic policy implications for the United States. The TPP is ambitious in at least four ways: (1) its size—it would be the largest U.S. FTA by trade flows and could expand in a region that represents over half of all U.S. trade; (2) the scope and scale of its liberalization—the parties, while not always at the desired level of ambition, have agreed to reduce barriers to goods, services, and agricultural trade and to establish rules and disciplines on a wide range of topics, including new policy issues that neither the WTO nor existing FTAs yet cover; (3) its potential evolution as a "living agreement"—it may continue to be expanded in terms of its membership and its rules and disciplines, and a number of countries officially have expressed an interest in joining TPP if it goes into effect; and (4) its geo-political significance—it has become, for some observers in the United States and Asia, a symbol of U.S. commitment to and influence in the Asia-Pacific, a region of growing economic and military importance where U.S. leadership increasingly is being challenged. As Congress debates potential implementing legislation, it has a wide and complex set of issues to consider.

APPENDIX

Table A-1. U.S. Goods Trade with TPP Countries, 2015 (in millions of U.S. dollars, ordered by total trade)

Country	Exports	Imports	Balance	Total Trade
Canada	280,017	295,190	-15,173	575,207
Mexico	236,377	294,741	-58,364	531,118
Japan	62,472	131,120	-68,648	193,592
Singapore	28,657	18,235	10,422	46,892
Malaysia	12,293	33,828	-21,535	46,121
Vietnam	7,072	37,993	-30,921	45,065
Australia	25,038	10,862	14,176	35,900
Chile	15,587	8,880	6,707	24,467
Peru	8,811	5,069	3,742	13,880
New Zealand	3,634	4,282	-648	7,916
Brunei	133	19	114	152
Total	680,091	840,219	-160,128	1,520,310

Source: U.S. International Trade Commission.

Notes: U.S. general imports, U.S. total exports.

Table A-2. U.S. Private Services Trade with TPP Countries, 2014 (in millions of U.S. dollars, ordered by total trade)

Country	Exports	Imports	Balance	Total Trade
Canada	61,353	30,074	31,279	91,427
Japan	46,698	31,237	15,461	77,935
Mexico	30,000	19,487	10,513	49,487
Australia	19,394	6,747	12,647	26,141
Singapore	11,941	5,964	5,977	17,905
Chile	3,813	1,227	2,586	5,040
Malaysia	2,859	1,789	1,070	4,648
New Zealand	2,216	1,457	759	3,673
Total	178,274	97,982	80,292	276,256

Source: Bureau of Economic Analysis, Interactive Tables for International Data.
Notes: BEA does not collect services trade data for every partner country.

Table A-3. U.S. Foreign Direct Investment (FDI) with TPP Countries, 2014 (in millions of U.S. dollars, ordered U.S. FDI Flow Abroad)

Country	U.S. FDI Abroad (Annual Flow)	U.S. FDI Abroad (Stock)	FDI in U.S. (Annual Flow)	FDI in U.S. (Stock)
Canada	19,847	386,121	21,116	261,247
Singapore	19,435	179,764	1,184	20,609
Australia	16,594	180,315	94	47,340
Mexico	9,311	107,825	2,421	17,710
Malaysia	1,719	14,357	239	809
Peru	1,215	6,486	-45	123
Chile	292	27,560	124	730
Vietnam	118	1,473	-104	-126
Brunei	-36	-6	(D)	(D)
New Zealand	-39	7,760	68	1,011
Japan	-7,303	108,068	33,765	372,800
Total	61,153	1,019,723	58,862	722,253

Source: Bureau of Economic Analysis, Interactive Tables for International Data.

Notes: Stock refers to the accumulated value of FDI, whereas flow refers to the value of incoming or outgoing FDI in a particular year. (D) denotes information suppressed to protect individual company data.

"THE MAY 10TH AGREEMENT"

On May 10, 2007, a bipartisan group of congressional leaders and the Bush Administration released a statement on agreed principles in four policy areas: worker rights, environment protection, intellectual property rights, and foreign investment. The principles were to be reflected in provisions in four U.S. FTAs—with Colombia, Panama, Peru, and South Korea. Regarding worker rights, the May 10th Agreement (the Agreement) required the United States and FTA partners to commit to enforcing the five international labor principles enshrined in the International Labour Organization's (ILO's) 1998 Declaration on Fundamental Principles and Rights At Work and that the commitment be enforceable under the FTA. These rights are the freedom of association, the effective recognition of the right to collective bargaining, the elimination of all forms of compulsory or forced labor, the effective abolition of child labor, and the elimination of discrimination in respect of employment and occupation.

The Agreement also required FTAs to adhere to seven major multilateral environmental agreements: The seven agreements are the Convention on International Trade in Endangered Species; the Montreal Protocol on Ozone Depleting Substances; the Convention on Marine Pollution; the Inter-American Tropical Tuna Convention; the Ramsar Convention on the Wetlands; the International Convention for the Regulation of Whaling; and the Convention on Conservation of Antarctic Marine Living Resources.

Furthermore, the parties are not to waive or otherwise derogate from their labor or environmental protection laws in a manner that would affect trade or investment with the FTA partner(s). In addition, the labor and environment provisions must be enforceable, if consultation and other avenues fail, through the same dispute settlement procedures that apply to the other provisions in the FTA.

The Agreement also required the FTAs to include provisions related to patents and approval of pharmaceuticals for marketing exclusivity with different requirements for developed and developing countries.

Specifically, the Agreement required provisions dealing with the effective period of data exclusivity—the restrictions on the use of test data produced for market approval by generic drug producers; patent extensions; linkage of marketing approval of generic drugs to determination of possible patent infringement; and reaffirmation of adherence to Doha Declaration on compulsory licensing of drugs to respond to public health crises.

Regarding foreign investment, the Agreement required each of the FTAs to state that none of its provisions would accord foreign investors greater substantive rights in terms of foreign investment protection than are accorded U.S. investors in the United States.

End Notes

[1] TPP negotiating parties include Australia, Brunei, Canada, Chile, Japan, Malaysia, Mexico, New Zealand, Peru, Singapore, the United States, and Vietnam.

[2] For more information on TPA see CRS In Focus IF10297, *TPP-Trade Promotion Authority (TPA) Timeline*, by Ian F. Fergusson; CRS Report RL33743, *Trade Promotion Authority (TPA) and the Role of Congress in Trade Policy*, by Ian F. Fergusson; and CRS Report R43491, *Trade Promotion Authority (TPA): Frequently Asked Questions*, by Ian F. Fergusson and Richard S. Beth.

[3] NAFTA is an FTA between the United States, Canada, and Mexico. For more information see CRS In Focus IF10047, *North American Free Trade Agreement (NAFTA)*, by M. Angeles Villarreal.

[4] See CRS In Focus IF10297, *TPP-Trade Promotion Authority (TPA) Timeline*, by Ian F. Fergusson and CRS Report R43491, *Trade Promotion Authority (TPA): Frequently Asked Questions*, by Ian F. Fergusson and Richard S. Beth.

[5] This section written by Ben Dolven and Brock Williams. For more information on the strategic aspects of TPP see CRS Report R44361, *The Trans-Pacific Partnership (TPP): Strategic Implications*, coordinated by Ben Dolven and Brock R. Williams.

[6] USTR, "Remarks by Ambassador Michael Froman at the Council on Foreign Relations: The Strategic Logic of Trade," June 16, 2014, http://www.ustr.gov/about-us/press-office/speeches/transcripts/2014/June/Remarks-USTR-Froman-at-Council-Foreign-Relations-Strategic-Logic-of-Trade.

[7] State Department, "Secretary's Remarks: U.S. Foreign Policy in a Changing World," October 17, 2015. http://www.state.gov/secretary/remarks/2015/10/248302.htm.

[8] Jonathan Soble, "Failure of Obama's Trans-Pacific Trade Deal Could Hurt U.S. Influence in Asia," *New York Times*, June 16, 2015.

[9] Jeffrey A. Bader and David Dollar, "Why the TPP Is the Linchpin of the Asia Rebalance," Brookings.edu, July 28, 2015.

[10] See, for instance, Prime Minister's Office of Singapore, "Transcript of Keynote Speech by Prime Minister Lee Hsien Loong at the Shangri-La Dialogue 29 May 2015." http://www.pmo.gov.sg/mediacentre/transcript-keynote-speech- prime-minister-lee-hsien-loong-shangri-la-dialogue-29-may-2015.

[11] Daniel Slane and Michael Wessel, "The TPP: Why It Won't Address Security Concerns with China," *Renewing America* blog, Council on Foreign Relations, May 15, 2015.

[12] White House, "Statement by the President on the Trans-Pacific Partnership," press release, October 5, 2015, https://www.whitehouse.gov/the-press-office/2015/10/05/statement-president-trans-pacific-partnership.

[13] Simon Lester, *Chinese Free Trade is No Threat to American Free Trade,* Cato Institute, April 22, 2015.

[14] For more information concerning the strategic aspects of TPP, CRS Report R44361, *The Trans-Pacific Partnership (TPP): Strategic Implications*, coordinated by Ben Dolven and Brock R. Williams.

[15] This section was written by James Jackson and Brock Williams, with assistance from Gabriel Nelson. For more information, see CRS Report R42344, *Trans-Pacific Partnership (TPP) Countries: Comparative Trade and Economic Analysis*, by Brock R. Williams.

[16] Sheila A. Smith, "Trans-Pacific Partnership Trade Deal," Council on Foreign Relations, event transcript, October 6, 2015, at http://www.cfr.org/asia-and-pacific/trans-pacific-partnership-trade-deal/p37091.

[17] For more information on trade and employment, see CRS In Focus IF10161, *International Trade Agreements and Job Estimates*, by James K. Jackson.

[18] Ben Bland and Shawn Donnan, "Vietnam looks for reform and investment boost from TPP deal," *Financial Times*, October 6, 2015.

[19] USITC, *TPP Agreement: Likely Impact on the U.S. Economy and on Specific Industry Sectors*, Publication 4607, May 2016.

[20] Peter Petri and Michael Plummer, "The Economic Effects of the Trans-Pacific Partnership: New Estimates," Peterson Institute for International Economics, January 2016, at http://piie.com/publications/wp/wp16-2.pdf.

[21] Dani Rodrik, "The Trade Numbers Game," Project Syndicate, blog post, February 10, 2016, at https://www.project-syndicate.org/commentary/tpp-debate-economic-benefits-by-dani-rodrik-2016-02.

[22] World Bank *Global Economic Prospects*, "Potential Implications of the Trans-Pacific Partnership Agreement," January 2016, at http://www.worldbank.org/en/publication/global-economic-prospects/GEP-Jan-2016-Implications- Trans-Pacific-Partnership.

[23] Robert Z. Lawrence and Tyler Moran, *Adjustment and Income Distribution Impacts of the Trans-Pacific Partnership*, Peterson Institute for International Economics, Working Paper WP 16-5, March 2016, at http://piie.com/publications/wp/wp16-5.pdf.

[24] Jeronim Capaldo and Alex Izurieta with Jomo Kwame Sundaram, "Trading Down: Unemployment, Inequality and Other Risks of the Trans-Pacific Partnership Agreement," Tufts University Global Development and Environment Institute, January 2016, at http://www.ase.tufts.edu/gdae/Pubs/wp/16-01Capaldo-IzurietaTPP.pdf.

[25] Robert Z. Lawrence, "Studies of TPP: Which is Credible?", *Trade and Investment Policy Watch*, Peterson Institute for International Economics, blog post, January 29, 2016, at blos.piie.com/trade/?p=553.

[26] According to the International Monetary Fund's October 2015 World Economic Outlook, both countries had a GDP growth rate of 6% in 2014. For the ten years prior, growth averaged 5% annually in Malaysia, and 6.4% annually in Vietnam.

[27] TPP accounts for a smaller share of U.S. services trade because of the large U.S.-EU services trade relationship.

[28] For more see CRS Report R42344, *Trans-Pacific Partnership (TPP) Countries: Comparative Trade and Economic Analysis*, by Brock R. Williams.

[29] The Uruguay Round agreement was signed in April 1994, nearly seven years after it was launched but less than a year after legislation implementing NAFTA was signed by the U.S. Congress.

[30] The 10 ASEAN members are Brunei, Burma (Myanmar), Cambodia, Indonesia, Laos, Malaysia, the Philippines, Singapore, Thailand, and Vietnam.

[31] In addition to the 12 TPP countries, APEC includes China, Hong Kong (officially Hong Kong, China), Indonesia, Papua New Guinea, the Philippines, Russia, South Korea, Taiwan (officially, Chinese Taipei), and Thailand.

[32] For more information see CRS In Focus IF10342, *What Is the Regional Comprehensive Economic Partnership?*, by Michael F. Martin et al.

[33] Asia-Pacific Economic Cooperation, *2015 Leaders' Declaration*, November 2015.

[34] "TPP Leaders Statement," November 2, 2011, https://ustr.gov/about-us/policy-offices/press-office/press- releases/2011/november/trans-pacific-partnership-leaders-statement.

[35] Business associations supporting the agreement include: U.S. Chamber of Commerce, National Association of Manufacturers, and the American Farm Bureau. Unions opposed to the agreement include: American Federation of Labor and Congress of Industrial Organizations (AFL-CIO), United Steelworkers (USW), and Teamsters. NGO's opposed to the agreement include: Doctors without Borders, Public Citizen, and Sierra Club.

[36] This section was written by Brock Williams and Gabriel Nelson.

[37] Updated tariff schedules have been posted by New Zealand, the depository for the TPP, at https://www.mfat.govt.nz/en/about-us/who-we-are/treaty-making-process/trans-pacific-partnership-tpp/text-of-the- trans-pacific-partnership.

[38] HS codes become increasingly disaggregated with each additional digit and are uniform across countries only up to 6 digits. Product descriptions in the TPP tariff schedules, which are at the 8-10 digit level, may vary by country.

[39] See U.S. staging categories, US17 and US24, in the U.S. General Notes to the Tariff Schedule in the TPP text.

[40] Caroline Freund, Tyler Moran, and Sarah Oliver, "Tariff Liberalization" in *Assessing the Trans-Pacific Partnership: Market Access and Sectoral Issues*, Peterson Institute for International Economics, PIIE Briefing 16-1, February 2016, p. 31, http://www.iie.com/publications/briefings/piieb16-1.pdf.

[41] Based on 2014 trade data from IMF DOTS.

[42] CRS analysis focuses on the share of liberalized tariff lines. This metric allows for comparison across countries and previous trade agreements, but it has limitations. In particular, each country has a unique number of tariff lines, which it determines, making the share of liberalization achieved, in effect, endogenous (i.e., a country can affect its liberalization share by changing the number of total tariff lines in its tariff schedule). Unique tariff lines range from just above 7,500 in New Zealand to more than 10,000 in the United States. Japanese tariff commitments are particularly complex among the TPP countries, including some cases with multiple tariffs associated with the same HTS code. In these cases, the authors' included only the least liberalized tariff in their calculations. Some HTS codes also appear to apply to only a subset of TPP countries. Those not applicable to the United States were excluded from the calculations. Finally, approximately 50 tariff lines in the Japanese schedule refer to non-originating goods, and were also excluded.

[43] USITC, *U.S.-Korea Free Trade Agreement: Potential Economy-wide and Selected Sectoral Effects*, Publication 3949, September 2007, p. 1-8.

[44] This section written by Vivian C. Jones, Specialist in International Trade and Finance.

[45] This section prepared by Michaela D. Platzer.

[46] American Apparel & Footwear Association (AAFA), "ApparelStats 2014 and ShoeStats 2014 Reports," press release, January 9, 2015, https:/www.wewear.org/apparelstats-2014-and-shoestats-2014-reports/.

[47] Ibid.

[48] Letter from Kevin M. Burke, President & Chief Executive Officer, AAFA, to Donald Evans, Secretary of Commerce, February 21, 2003. In the TPP, these footwear types include 18 items such as certain waterproof footwear with rubber or plastic soles that are glued together (Harmonized Tariff Schedule (HTS) 6401.10.00) and sports and certain athletic footwear with outer soles of rubber or plastics, valued over $12 per pair (HTS 6402.91.990).

The Footwear Distributors and Retailers of America (FDRA) describes the specific sensitive tariff lines in its TPP Footwear Duty Guidebook.

[49] Import data are from the Department of Commerce's Office of Textiles and Apparel (OTEXA), accessed February 22, 2016.

[50] OTEXA, Vietnam, U.S. Export Markets, February 22, 2016, http://otexa.trade.gov/ exports/ e5520.htm.

[51] The majority of yarns and fabrics exported from the United States are sold to Canada and Mexico (TPP partners), CAFTA-DR countries, and Peru and Colombia, South American FTA partners.

[52] CRS Report R42772, *U.S. Textile Manufacturing and the Trans-Pacific Partnership Negotiations*, by Michaela D. Platzer.

[53] The United States negotiated special rules for certain textile, apparel, and footwear products to account for different tariff rates and prevent circumvention of high tariffs in some TPP countries. See, U.S. Appendix C, Tariff Differentials, https://ustr.gov/sites/default/files/ TPP-Final-Text-US-Appendix-C-Tariff-Differentials.pdf.

[54] USITC, *TPP Agreement: Likely Impact on the U.S. Economy and on Specific Industry Sectors*, Publication 4607, May 2016, pp. 254, 273.

[55] See, Letter from Ambassador Michael B.G. Froman, United States Trade Representative, to Vu Huy Hoang, Minister of Trade and Industry, November 2015, https://ustr.gov/sites/default/ files/TPP-Final-Text-Labour-US-VN-Plan-for-Enhancement-of-Trade-and-Labor-Relations.pdf.

[56] The yarn-forward rule of origin is included in most US FTAs, such as NAFTA, CAFTA-DR, and agreements with Australia, Chile, Colombia, Panama, Peru, and Singapore.

[57] The RVC test for footwear requires TPP content of 45% using the build-up rule or 55% using the build-down method. The calculation includes labor, material, and manufacturing costs.

[58] Eight of the 187 items will only be on the short supply list for 5 years after the agreement takes effect.

[59] OTEXA, *The Transpacific Partnership (TPP): An Overview of the Rules of Origin and Market Access Commitments for Textiles and Apparel*, February 2, 2016, pp. 15-16, http://otexa.trade.gov/PDFs/OTEXA_Webinar_TPP_Feb_2016.pdf.

[60] Similar programs are included in the CAFTA-DR FTA and Haiti Trade Preference Programs. The TPP program is detailed in Appendix E of the U.S. tariff schedule applicable to imports from TPP member states, https://ustr.gov/sites/default/files/TPP-Final-Text-US-Appendix-E-Earned-Import-Allowance-Program.pdf.

[61] Rachel Horowitz, Nicole Lorden, and Sophie Miyashiro, *Best Practices Manual: How to Import Cotton Apparel Under the Dominican Republic-Central America-United States Free Trade Agreement (CAFTA-DR)*, Fashion Institute of Technology, March 2013, p. 5.

[62] Industry Trade Advisory Committee (ITAC 13) on Textiles and Clothing on the Trans-Pacific Partnership Agreement, December 2, 2015, https://ustr.gov/sites/default/files/ITAC-13-Textiles-and-Clothing.pdf.

[63] Ibid., p. 5.

[64] NCTO, "U.S. Textile Manufacturers Endorse Trans-Pacific Partnership," press release, January 21, 2016, http://www.ncto.org/category/press-releases/.

[65] See, AAFA, "Apparel & Footwear Association Releases Statement of Support for the Trans-Pacific Partnership," press release, February 1, 2016, and Footwear Distributors and Retailers of America (FDRA), "Pre-hearing Statement for the public hearing on the Trans-Pacific Partnership: Likely Impact on the U.S. Economy and on Specific Industry Sectors," p. 10, December 21, 2015.

[66] See, Rose Marcario, "Patagonia Opposes TPP," Patagonia, November 13, 2015, http://www.thecleanestline.com/2015/11/patagonia-opposes-tpp.html and "New Balance renews opposition to TPP," by Matthew Korade, Politico Pro, April 12, 2015.

[67] This section prepared by Bill Canis.

[68] Automotive News, *Data Center*, U.S. Car and Light-Truck Sales by Make, 2014, January 5, 2015.

[69] Vehicles are exported from U.S. plants not only by General Motors, Ford, and Fiat-Chrysler, but also by Japanese, German, and Korean automakers. U.S. Department of Commerce, Office of Transportation and Machinery, *Trends in U.S. Vehicle Exports*, August 2015, pp. 4 and 6. http://trade.gov/mas/manufacturing/OAAI/build/groups/ public/@tg_oaai/ documents/webcontent/tg_oaai_004086.pdf.

[70] Ibid., p. 9.

[71] Other major non-TPP export markets (in terms of units sold) for U.S. vehicles in 2014 were China (307,425), Germany (147,680), and Saudi Arabia (104,074).

[72] USITC, *TPP Agreement: Likely Impact on the U.S. Economy and on Specific Industry Sectors*, Publication 4607, May 2016, pp. 232.

[73] For six TPP countries (Australia, Canada, Chile, Mexico, Peru, and Singapore, with which the United States already has FTAs), the TPP vehicle duties are zero when the agreement takes effect. For Brunei, Malaysia, and New Zealand, vehicle duties are cut in half when the agreement takes effect with the remaining duty removed in year 13 of the agreement. Vietnam will also remove most auto tariffs by year 13 of the agreement, but tariffs on used vehicles (representing nearly one-third of Vietnam's auto tariff lines) will remain in place.

[74] *ITAC 2 Advisory Committee Report to the President, the Congress, and the United States Trade Representative on the Trans Pacific Partnership Trade Agreement*, December 22, 2015, p. 5.

[75] Sarah Oliver, *Assessing the Trans-Pacific Partnership: Auto Sector Liberalization*, Peterson Institute for International Economics, PIIE Briefing 16-1, February 2016, p. 60, http://www.piie.com/publications/briefings/piieb16-1.pdf.

[76] Motor Vehicle Trade Appendix between United States and Japan, available at https://ustr.gov/sites/default/files/TPP- Final-Text-Japan-Appendix-D-Appendix-between-Japan-and-the-United-States-on-Motor-Vehicle-Trade.pdf; Also see U.S.-Japan letter exchange, https://ustr.gov/sites/default/files/TPP-Final-Text-US-JP-Letter-Exchange-on-Certain-Auto-NTMs.pdf; and https://ustr.gov/sites/default/files/TPP-Final-Text-JP-to-US-Letter-on-Motor-Vehicle- Distribution-Survey.pdf.

[77] In the U.S.-Korea FTA several types of content calculations are allowed: for both vehicles and parts: 35% (net cost) or 55% (build down).

[78] ITAC 2, p. 7.

[79] Supporters of the TPP agreement include: Toyota North America, Honda North America, Association of Global Automakers, and Motor and Equipment Manufacturers Association.

[80] Industry Trade Advisory Committee on Automotive Equipment and Capital Goods, *ITAC 2 Advisory Committee Report.*

[81] Ford Motor Company has announced its opposition to TPP and also publicly announced in January 2016 that it was withdrawing from the Japanese (and Indonesian) markets, stating that in those markets it does not see a "path to profitability" and that "market dynamics prevent us from being competitive. Ford's press release also singled out the TPP's effect: "Japan is the most closed, developed auto economy in the world, with all imported brands accounting for less than 6% of Japan's annual new car market. The overall industry in Japan is projected to decline in coming years, leaving even less opportunity for success. In addition, in its current form, the Trans Pacific Partnership will not materially improve our ability to compete effectively in the market." Ford Motor Company, "Ford Announces Closure of Operations in Japan and Indonesia Later This Year," press release, January 25, 2016, http://www.at.ford.com/news/cn/Pages/Important%20Announcement.aspx.

[82] See the UAW press release outlining its reasons for opposition. International Union, United Automobile, Aerospace and Agricultural Implement Workers of America (UAW), "United Auto Workers Leadership Statement of Opposition to the TPP—Statement from UAW President Williams," press release, December 3, 2015, http://uaw.org/united-auto- workers-leadership-statement-of-opposition-to-the-tpp-statement-from-uaw-president-williams/.

[83] ITAC 2 report, p. 17.

[84] Ibid., p. 8.

[85] Ibid., p. 15.

[86] Sarah Oliver, *Assessing the Trans-Pacific Partnership: Auto Sector Liberalization,* p. 65.

[87] ITAC 2, p. 5.

[88] CRS calculations based on the legally verified TPP Tariff Elimination Schedules.

[89] ITAC 2, p. 7.

[90] ITAC 2, p. 14.

[91] This section written by Rachel Fefer and Brock Williams.

[92] For more information see CRS Report R43291, *U.S. Trade in Services: Trends and Policy Issues*, by Rachel F. Fefer.

[93] Meredith M. Broadbent, Chairman, *Recent Trends in U.S. Services Trade: 2015 Annual Report*, United States International Trade Commission, May 2015, http://www.usitc.gov/publications/332/pub4526.pdf.

[94] David Autor, David Dorn, and Gordon H. Hanson, "Why Obama's Key Trade Deal with Asia Would Actually be Good for American Workers," *Washington Post*, March 12, 2015.

[95] For more information see CRS Report R43387, *Transatlantic Trade and Investment Partnership (T-TIP) Negotiations*, by Shayerah Ilias Akhtar, Vivian C. Jones, and Renée Johnson; and CRS In Focus IF10311, *Trade in Services Agreement (TiSA) Negotiations*, by Rachel F. Fefer.

[96] OECD Services Trade Restrictiveness Index available at http://www.oecd.org/tad/services-trade/services-trade- restrictiveness-index.htm.

[97] Ingo Borchert, Batshur Gootiiz, and Aaditya Mattoo, *Policy Barriers to International Trade in Services: New Empirical Evidence*, World Bank Policy Research Working Paper (WPS6109), 2012, http://iresearch.worldbank.org/ servicetrade/home.htm.

[98] USITC, *TPP Agreement: Likely Impact on the U.S. Economy and on Specific Industry Sectors*, Publication 4607, May 2016, pp. 319.

[99] Leo Lewis, "Yamato Launches Rare Japan Post Broadside," *Financial Times*, November 12, 2015.

[100] Industry Trade Advisory Committee on Services and Finance Industries (ITAC 10), *Advisory Committee Report to the President, the Congress and the U.S. Trade Representative on the Trans-Pacific Partnership Trade Agreement*, December 3, 2015.

[101] See TPP Annex 11-A for a complete listing of insurance, banking, and other financial services covered by the cross- border trade in financial services disciplines.

[102] Ambassador Peter Allgeier, *Testimony before the International Trade Commission*, Coalition of Services Industries, January 14, 2016, https://servicescoalition.org/images/CSI_Public_Documents/ITC_Hearing_on_Economic_Impact_of_TPP_on_Service s.pdf.

[103] ITAC 10, op. cit.; Letter from Representative Mike Kelley, Member of Congress, et al. to Jacob J. Lew, Treasury Secretary, et al., January 11, 2016; Letter from Senator Kelly Ayotte, Member of Congress, et al. to Jacob J. Lew, Treasury Secretary, et al., March 7, 2016.

[104] U.S. Congress, House Committee on Appropriations, Subcommittee on Financial Services and General Government, *President Obama's Fiscal 2017 Budget Request for the Treasury Department*, 114th Cong., 2nd sess., March 16, 2016.

[105] Treasury Department, *A New Approach to Data Localization and Financial Services*, May 26, 2016.

[106] This letter can be found at https://ustr.gov/sites/default/files/TPP-Final-Text-US-JP-Letter-Exchange-on-Non-Tariff- Measures.pdf.

[107] USTR, *TPP Chapter Summary: Temporary Entry for Business Persons*, November 5, 2016, at https://ustr.gov/sites/default/files/TPP-Chapter-Summary-Temporary-Entry-for-Business-Persons.pdf.

[108] See annex 12-A of the TPP text.

[109] USTR, *TPP Chapter Summary: Telecommunications*, November 5, 2016, at https://ustr.gov/sites/default/files/TPP- Chapter-Summary-Telecommunications.pdf; and Industry Trade Advisory Committee for Information and Communications Technologies, Services and Electronic Commerce (ITAC 8), *Advisory Committee Report to the President, the Congress and the U.S. Trade Representative on the Trans-Pacific Partnership Trade Agreement*, December 3, 2015.

[110] ITAC 10, op. cit.

[111] Allgeier, op. cit.

[112] Allgeier, op. cit.

[113] "Administration Engages with Financial Services Firms on TPP Objections," *Inside U.S. Trade*, December 4, 2015.

[114] Letter from Representative Mike Kelley, Member of Congress, et al. to Jacob J. Lew, Treasury Secretary, et al., January 11, 2016; Letter from Senator Kelly Ayotte, Member of Congress, et al. to Jacob J. Lew, Treasury Secretary, et al., March 7, 2016.

[115] ITAC 10, op. cit.

[116] CWA, "10 Ways the TPP Would Hurt U.S. Working Families," accessed April 22, 2016, at http://www.cwa- nion.org/pages/10_ways_the_tpp_would_hurt_cwa_represented_workers.

[117] Public Citizen, "The Trans-Pacific Partnership: Undermining Wall Street Reform," April 22, 2016, at http://www.citizen.org/Page.aspx?pid=6474.

[118] This section written by Mark McMinimy.

[119] Under a TRQ, lower tariffs are applied to in-quota imports, while higher, often prohibitive tariffs are imposed on imports in excess of the quota amount.

[120] The MFN rate is the normal nondiscriminatory tariff charged on imports from WTO members, excluding preferential tariffs under free trade agreements and other schemes, or tariffs charged inside quota regimes.

[121] World Tariff Profiles 2015, World Trade Organization, at https://www.wto.org/english/res_e/booksp_e/tariff_profiles15_e.pdf.

[122] USITC, *TPP Agreement: Likely Impact on the U.S. Economy and on Specific Industry Sectors*, Publication 4607, May 2016, pp. 111.

[123] For more information on GIs, see CRS In Focus IF10188, *Geographical Indications (GIs) in U.S.-EU Trade Negotiations*, by Renée Johnson.

[124] For more information on SPS, see CRS Report R43450, *Sanitary and Phytosanitary (SPS) and Related Non-Tariff Barriers to Agricultural Trade*, by Renée Johnson.

[125] Modern biotechnology is defined in the TPP text as the application of: (a) in vitro nucleic acid techniques, including recombinant deoxyribonucleic acid (rDNA) and direct injection of nucleic acid into cells or organelles, or (b) fusion of cells beyond the taxonomic family. Such products are also sometimes referred to as genetically engineered, or more popularly, genetically modified organisms (GMOs).

[126] APAC report of December 1, 2015, at https://ustr.gov/trade-agreements/free-trade-agreements/trans-pacific- partnership/advisory-group-reports-TPP.

[127] Public Citizen, "The Trans-Pacific Partnership: Undermining Food Safety," accessed April 22, 2016, at http://www.citizen.org/tpp-food-safety-facts.

[128] Briefing Note: Government Procurement Agreement, http://www.wto.org/english/thewto_e/minist_e/min11_e/ brief_gpa_e.htm.

[129] For more information, see CRS Report R43140, *The Buy American Act—Preferences for "Domestic" Supplies: In Brief*, by Kate M. Manuel.

[130] U.S. manufactured products have been defined in regulation as containing at least 50% domestic content.

[131] SDR (special drawing right) refers to an International Monetary Fund (IMF) international reserve asset. Its value is based on the U.S. dollar, euro, yen, and pound sterling, and will be expanded to include the Chinese Renminbi (RMB) in October 2016.

[132] Written by Shayerah Ilias Akhtar (x7-9253) and Ian F. Fergusson (x7-4997), Specialists in International Trade and Finance. See CRS Report RL34292, *Intellectual Property Rights*

and International Trade, by Shayerah Ilias Akhtar and Ian F. Fergusson, and CRS In Focus IF10033, *Intellectual Property Rights (IPR) and International Trade*, by Shayerah Ilias Akhtar and Ian F. Fergusson.

[133] CRS calculation based on data from U.S. Bureau of Economic Analysis (BEA), U.S. Trade in Services; U.S. trade in IP services data available for selected TPP countries (Australia, Canada, Chile, Japan, Mexico, New Zealand, and Singapore).

[134] For a description of the econometric model and assumptions made, see USITC, *TPP Agreement: Likely Impact on the U.S. Economy and on Specific Industry Sectors*, Publication 4607, May 2016, pp. 475-478.

[135] USTR, *2015 Special 301 Report*, April 2015, https://ustr.gov/sites/default/files/2015-Special-301-Report- FINAL.pdf.

[136] For an overview of this discussion, see WTO, WIPO, and WHO, *Promoting Access to Medical Technologies and Innovation: Intersections Between Public Health, Intellectual Property, and Trade, 2013*, https:/www.wto.org/english/res_e/booksp_e/pamtiwhowipowtoweb13_e.pdf. See also, TPP Issues Analysis: Access to Medicines, Ways and Means Democrats Forum on Access to Medicine, December 8, 2015, testimonies of Joe Damond Biotechnology Industry Assocciation; Rohit Malpani, Médecins Sans Frontières; Stephen Ezell, Information Technology and Innovation (ITIF) Foundation; and Peter Maybarduk, Global Citizen, available at http://democrats.waysandmeans.house.gov/trading-views-real-debates-key-issues-tpp.

[137] "The Trans-Pacific Partnership Agreement: Report of the Industry Trade Advisory Committee on Intellectual Property Rights (ITAC-15)", December 3, 2015.

[138] KORUS provided 4 years from filing.

[139] Biologics are drugs made from living organisms.

[140] For more information on biologics, see CRS Report R44032, *Patents and Regulatory Exclusivities: Issues in Pharmaceutical Innovation and Competition*, by John R. Thomas; and CRS Report R44173, *Follow-On Biologics: Intellectual Property Issues*, by John R. Thomas.

[141] "Trade Talks Stumble Over Biologics Data Exclusivity," *Regulatory Focus,* February 11, 2015, http://www.raps.org/Regulatory-Focus/News/2015/02/11/21309/Trade-Talks-Stumble-over-Biologics-Data- Exclusivity/#sthash.QopagH5c.dpuf.

[142] "White House Must Fix Biologics to Move TPP, Hatch Says," *International Trade Reporter*, April 7, 2016. Meanwhile, the Administration in its 2017 budget request maintains its preference for a 7-year exclusivity period in calculating budget costs.

[143] Australian Department of Foreign Affairs and Trade, "Outcomes: Biologics," fact sheet, http://dfat.gov.au/trade/agreements/tpp/outcomes-documents/Pages/outcomes-biologics.aspx.

[144] The WIPO Copyright Treaty and WIPO Performances and Phonograms Treaty are known as the WIPO "Internet Treaties."

[145] In 2015, Canada extended copyright protection to 70 years to rights of performers (singers and musicians) and makers of sound recordings (record companies).

[146] USTR, TPP—"Promoting Digital Trade," https://ustr.gov/sites/default/files/TPP-Promoting-Digital-Trade-Fact- Sheet.pdf.

[147] for example, the American Society of Composers, Authors, and Publishers (ASCAP), or Broadcast Music Inc. (BMI).

[148] For more information on these marks, see WIPO, "Certification Marks," http://www.wipo.int/sme/en/ip_business/collective_marks/certification_marks.htm; and WIPO, "Collective Marks," http://www.wipo.int/sme/en/ip_business/collective_ marks/collective_marks.htm.

[149] Written by Shayerah Ilias Akhtar and Ian F. Fergusson. See CRS Report R44015, *International Investment Agreements (IIAs): Frequently Asked Questions*, coordinated by Martin A. Weiss; and CRS In Focus IF10052, *U.S. International Investment Agreements (IIAs)*, by Martin A. Weiss and Shayerah Ilias Akhtar.

[150] The investment chapter of the U.S. FTA with Australia, however, does not contain investor-state dispute settlement.

[151] Australian Government, Attorney-General's Department, "Tobacco Plain Packaging—Investor-State Arbitration," https://www.ag.gov.au/tobaccoplainpackaging; and Philip Morris International, "Philip Morris Asia Limited Comments on Tribunal's Decision to Decline Jurisdiction in Arbitration Against Commonwealth of Australia over Plain Packaging," December 17, 2015, http://investors.pmi.com/phoenix.zhtml?c=146476&p=irol- newsArticle&ID=2123843.

[152] TransCanada, "Trans-Canada Commences Legal Action Following Keystone XL Denial," press release, January 6, 2016, http://www.transcanada.com/announcements-article.html?id=2014960.

[153] CRS Report R43988, *Issues in International Trade: A Legal Overview of Investor-State Dispute Settlement*, by Brandon J. Murrill and Daniel T. Shedd.

[154] Based on its available data, the United Nations Conference on Trade and Development (UNCTAD) reported that, at the end of 2014, the overall (cumulative) number of concluded ISDS cases reached 356, of which about 37% were decided in favor of the state (all claims dismissed either on jurisdictional grounds or on the merits), 25% were decided in favor of the investor (monetary compensation awarded), 28% were settled, 8% were discontinued, and 2% where a treaty breach was found but no monetary compensation was awarded to the investor. See UNCTAD, Investor-State Dispute Settlement: Review of Developments in 2014, IIA Issues Note No. 2, May 2015, p. 5, http://investmentpolicyhub.unctad.org/Upload/Documents/UNCTAD_WEB_DIAE_PCB_2015_%202%20IIA%20ISS UES%20NOTES%2013MAY%20.pdf.

[155] See http://trade.ec.europa.eu/doclib/docs/2015/november/tradoc_153955.pdf.

[156] European Commission, "EU-Vietnam Free Trade Agreement Now Available Online," press release, February 1, 2016.

[157] European Commission, "CETA: EU and Canada Agree on New Approach on Investment in Trade Agreements," press release, February 29, 2016.

[158] For example, see Letter from Committee of Chairs, Industry Trade Advisory Committee (ITAC) to Penny Pritzker, Secretary of Commerce, and Michael Froman, U.S. Trade Representative, November 20, 2015.

[159] For example, see testimony of Matthew C. Porterfield, "The Investment Chapter of the Trans-Pacific Partnership," for House Ways & Means Committee Democrats' "Trading Views: Real Debate on Key Issues in TPP" Hearing on Investment, December 2, 2015.

[160] USTR, TPP Investment Chapter Summary, p. 3, https://ustr.gov/sites/default/files/TPP-Chapter-Summary- Investment.pdf.

[161] USTR, "TPP: Upgrading & Improving Investor-State Dispute Settlement," https://ustr.gov/sites/default/files/TPP- Upgrading-and-Improving-Investor-State-Dispute-Settlement-Fact-Sheet.pdf.

[162] For example, see Porterfield testimony.

[163] KORUS had this provision, but gave the tribunal greater deference as to whether to accept them.

[164] For discussion of the view that TPP's ISDS improves upon previous agreements, see Gary Clyde Hufbauer, "Investor-State Dispute Settlement," in Peterson Institute for International Economics, *Assessing the Trans-Pacific Partnership, Volume 1: Market Access and Sectoral Issues*, PIIE Briefing 16-1, February 2016.

[165] *Inside U.S. Trade*, USTR Claims Variety of Upgrades to ISDS in TPP, But Details Still Unclear, October 14, 2015.

[166] See, for instance, testimony of Theodore R. Posner, for House Ways and Means Committee Democrats, "Trading Views: Real Debates on Key Issues in TPP - Investment Chapter," December 2, 2015.

[167] The FCTC entered into force on February 27, 2005. The United States is one of the 168 signatories, but has not ratified it.

[168] For example, see "Tobacco Opponents, Advocates Fight for USTR's Favor on TPP Carveout," *Inside U.S. Trade*, August 7, 2015, which discusses various letters sent by Members of Congress to USTR on the issue of the tobacco carveout from TPP. See also Thomas J. Bollyky, "The War on Tobacco Makes it into the TPP Free Trade Deal," *Newsweek*, February 13, 2016, http://www.newsweek.com/war-tobacco-makes-it-tpp-free-trade-deal-426206.

[169] Drawing from TPP's "investment agreement" definition (Art 9.1), an example of an investment agreement could be a written agreement concluded and signed after TPP's entry into force between the central government authority of one TPP party with the investor of another TPP party that is binding, on which the investor relies to establish or acquire an investment, and that grants right related to: natural resources that the authority controls, supplying services, or infrastructure projects.

[170] For further discussion, see Letter from Committee of Chairs, Industry Trade Advisory Committee (ITAC) to Penny Pritzker, Secretary of Commerce, and Michael Froman, U.S. Trade Representative, November 20, 2015. For details on Mexico, see USTR, National Trade Estimate (NTE) Report, March 2016, p. 305.

[171] NTE Report, p.284.

[172] Written by M. Angeles Villarreal and Ian F. Fergusson.

[173] For more information, see CRS Report RS22823, *Overview of Labor Enforcement Issues in Free Trade Agreements*, by Mary Jane Bolle; and CRS In Focus IF10046, *Worker Rights Provisions in Free Trade Agreements (FTAs)*, by Mary Jane Bolle and Ian F. Fergusson.

[174] Richard Trumka, "TPP: A New Low," *The Hill*, February 2, 2016.

[175] U.S. Congress, House Committee on Ways and Means, *TPP Issue Analysis: Worker Rights*, 114th Cong., February 1, 2016.

[176] Office of the United States Trade Representative, "U.S. Trade Representative Michael Froman Promotes Trans- Pacific Partnership at Consumer Electronics Show," press release, January 2016, https://ustr.gov/about-us/policy- offices/press-office/press-releases/2016/january/us-trade-representative-michael.

[177] The White House, Office of the press Secretary, "Statement by the President on the Signing of the Trans-Pacific Partnership," press release, February 3, 2016, https://www.whitehouse.gov/the-press-office/2016/02/03/statement- president-signing-trans-pacific-partnership.

[178] CRS In Focus IF10166, *Environmental Provisions in Free Trade Agreements (FTAs)*, by Richard K. Lattanzio and Ian F. Fergusson.

[179] In the end, the U.S. position supporting recourse to dispute settlement prevailed.

[180] The seven MEAS are: the Conventional on International Trade in Endangered Species of Wild Fauna and Flora (CITES), the Montreal Protocol on Substances that Deplete the Ozone Layer, International Convention for the Prevention of Pollution from Ships (MARPOL), the Convention on Wetlands of International Importance (Ramsar convention), Convention on the Conservation of Antarctic Marine Living Resources (CAMLR); International Convention on the Regulation of Whaling, Convention for the Establishment of an Inter-American Tropical Tuna Commission.

[181] As defined by the WTO's Agreement on Subsidies and Countervailing Measures.

[182] This section written by Rachel Fefer. For more information, see CRS In Focus IF10390, *TPP: Digital Trade Provisions*, by Rachel F. Fefer.

[183] James Manyika, et al, *Digital globalization: The new era of global flows*, February 2016, p. 30, http://www.mckinsey.com/business-functions/mckinsey-digital/our-insights/digital-globalization-the-new-era-of- global-flows?cid=other-eml-alt-mgi-mck-oth-1602.

[184] Department of Commerce Economics and Statistics Administration, *Digitally Deliverable Services Remain an Important Component of U.S. Trade*, May 28, 2015, http://www.esa.doc.gov/economic-briefings/digitally-deliverable- services-remain-important-component-us-trade.

[185] Industry Trade Advisory Committee on Information and Communication Technologies, Services, and Electronic Commerce (ITAC 8), *Advisory Committee Report to the President, the Congress and the USTR on the TPP Trade Agreement*, December 3, 2015, https://ustr.gov/sites/default/files/ITAC-8-Information-and-Communication- Technologies-Services-and-Electronic-Commerce.pdf.

[186] Steve Wilhelm, "Microsoft: TPP trade pact puts 'line in the sand' against digital protectionism," *Puget Sound Business Journal*, November 9, 2015.

[187] ITAC 10, op cit.

[188] See for example, https://www.eff.org/issues/tpp.

[189] Przemyslaw Kowalski et al., *State-Owned Enterprises Trade Effects and Policy Implications*, OECD, OECD Trade Policy Papers No. 147, 2013, http://dx.doi.org/10.1787/5k4869ckqk7l-en.

[190] General Statistics Office, *Statistical Handbook of Vietnam*, 2014, p. 88, www.gso.gov.vn/default_en.aspx?tabid=515&idmid=5&ItemID=14278.

[191] For example, see Linda M. Dempsey, *Pre-Hearing Statement before the USITC Hearing on Investigation No. TPA-105-001*, National Association of Manufacturers, January 8, 2016, p. 9.

[192] For example, see the ITAC 12 report. Industry Trade Advisory Committee on Steel, *Advisory Committee Report to the President, the Congress and the USTR on the TPP*, ITAC-12 Report, December 3, 2015, p. 11, https://ustr.gov/sites/default/files/ITAC-12-Steel.pdf.

[193] Derek Scissors, *Grading the Trans-Pacific Partnership on Trade*, American Enterprise Institute, December 2015, p. 6, https://www.aei.org/publication/grading-the-trans-pacific-partnership-on-trade/.

[194] For instance, the agreement states that Singapore's government must ensure that any government enterprise "acts solely in accordance with commercial considerations in its purchase or sale of goods or services" and that Singapore must make public a listing of organizations that satisfy the agreement's definition of a "covered entity," essentially any company organized in Singapore above a certain size and with a sufficient level of government influence. This list is also to include the ownership structure of the organization, members of government that serve on the board of directors, and total revenue or assets; USTR, *United States-Singapore Free Trade Agreement*, May 2003, pp. 133-140, http://www.ustr.gov/sites/default/files/uploads/agreements/fta/singapore/asset_upload_file708_4036.pdf.

[195] A similar provision has been included in previous FTAs, but in most cases, except the Singapore FTA, focused only on SOE sales to covered investments within that party's territory, excluding cross-border transactions and SOE purchases.

[196] SDR (special drawing right) refers to an International Monetary Fund (IMF) international reserve asset. Its value is based on the U.S. dollar, euro, yen, and pound sterling, and will be expanded to include the Chinese Renminbi (RMB) in October 2016.

[197] This section prepared by Rebecca M. Nelson. For more information about current debates over exchange rates, see CRS Report R43242, *Current Debates over Exchange Rates: Overview and Issues for Congress*, by Rebecca M. Nelson, and CRS In Focus IF10049, *Debates over "Currency Manipulation"*, by Rebecca M. Nelson.

[198] See Department of the Treasury website: http://www.treasury.gov/initiatives/Pages/joint-declaration.aspx.

[199] USTR, "Regulatory Coherence," https://medium.com/the-trans-pacific-partnership/regulatory-coherence-6672076f307a#.yeuk3p4r1

[200] A formulary is a list of medicines approved for prescription under a medical plan.

[201] USTR, *2015 National Trade Estimate Report on Foreign Trade Barriers*, p. 281.

[202] Evdokia Moise and Silvia Sorescu, *Trade Facilitation Indicators: The Potential Impact of Trade Facilitation on Developing Countries' Trade*, OECD, OECD Trade Policy Papers No. 144, 2013, http://dx.doi.org/10.1787/5k4bw6kg6ws2-en.

[203] Industry Trade Advisory Committee on Customs Matters and Trade Facilitation (ITAC 14), *Advisory Committee Report to the President, the Congress and the U.S. Trade Representative on the Trans-Pacific Partnership Trade Agreement*, December 3, 2015.

[204] For the full text, see https://ustr.gov/sites/default/files/TPP-Final-Text-Customs-Administration-and-Trade- Facilitation.pdf.

[205] "United Nations Convention against Corruption: Signature and Ratification Status as of 1 December 2015," United Nations Office on Drugs and Crime, https://www.unodc.org/unodc/en/treaties/CAC/signatories.html.

[206] USAID, Trade Capacity Building Database, February 17, 2016, https://eads.usaid.gov/tcb/.

[207] The trade statistics in this section come from: U.S. Census Bureau, Department of Commerce, *A Profile of U.S. Importing and Exporting Companies, 2012-2013*, CB15-51, April 7, 2015, https://www.census.gov/foreign-trade/Press- Release/edb/2013/edbrel.pdf. Percentages reflect share of total "identified" trade. Not all U.S. exports and imports can be matched to specific companies. In 2009, this "unidentified" trade accounted for 11% of exports and 12% of imports.

[208] Firm and employment share data from U.S. Census Bureau, Department of Commerce, *Statistics of U.S. Businesses: Statistics about Business Size*, http://www.census.gov/econ/ smallbus.html#RcptSize.

[209] David Neumark, Brandon Wall, and Junfu Zhang, "Do Small Businesses Create More Jobs? New Evidence for the United States from the National Establishment Time Series," *Review of Economics and Statistics*, vol. 93, no. 1 (February 2011), pp. 16-29; John C. Haltiwanger, Ron S. Jarmin, and Javier Miranda, "Who Creates Jobs? Small vs. Large vs. Young," *Review of Economics and Statistics*, vol. 95, no. 2 (May 2013), pp.347-361.

[210] These reports can be found at http://www.usitc.gov/research_and_analysis/ small_med_ enterprises.htm.

[211] USITC, *Small and Medium-Sized Enterprises: U.S. and EU Export Activities, and Barriers and Opportunities Experienced by U.S. Firms*, Investigation No. 332-509, USITC Publication 4169, July 2010, pp. 3-27.

[212] Advisory Committee for Trade Policy and Negotiations (ACTPN), *ACTPN Report to the President, the Congress, and the United States Trade Representative on the Trans-Pacific Partnership (TPP)*, December 3, 2015.

In: The Trans-Pacific Partnership
Editor: Derek Pierce

ISBN: 978-1-53610-195-9

Chapter 2

THE TRANS-PACIFIC PARTNERSHIP (TPP): STRATEGIC IMPLICATIONS*

Brock R. Williams, Ben Dolven, Ian F. Fergusson, Mark E. Manyin, Michael F. Martin and Wayne M. Morrison

SUMMARY

On February 4, 2016, Ministers of the 12 countries participating in the Trans Pacific Partnership (TPP) negotiations signed the proposed free trade agreement (FTA). TPP is one of the Obama Administration's signature trade policy initiatives, an effort to reduce and eliminate trade and investment barriers and establish new rules and disciplines to govern trade and investment among the 12 countries. TPP proponents, including Administration officials, argue that the proposed TPP would have substantial strategic benefits for the United States in addition to its direct economic impact. They argue that the agreement would enhance overall U.S. influence in the economically dynamic Asia-Pacific region and advance U.S. leadership in setting and modernizing the rules of commerce in the region and potentially in the multilateral trading system under the World Trade Organization (WTO).

---

* This is an edited, reformatted and augmented version of a Congressional Research Service publication R44361, prepared for Members and Committees of Congress, dated February 4, 2016.

Congress plays a key role in the TPP. Through U.S. trade negotiating objectives established in Trade Promotion Authority (TPA) legislation and informal consultations and oversight, Congress has guided the Administration's negotiations. Ultimately, Congress would need to pass implementing legislation if the concluded agreement is to take effect in the United States.

The geo-political arguments surrounding TPP are widely debated, as are the arguments about its potential economic impact. To some, the TPP is an important litmus test of U.S. credibility in the Asia-Pacific region. As the leading economic component of the Administration's "strategic rebalancing" to the region, the TPP, proponents argue, would allow the United States to reaffirm existing alliances, expand U.S. soft power, spur countries to adopt a more U.S.-friendly foreign policy outlook, and enhance broader diplomatic and security relations. Many Asian policymakers—correctly or not—could interpret a failure of TPP in the United States as a symbol of the United States' declining interest in the region and inability to assert leadership.

Some critics argue that TPP backers often do not identify specific, concrete ways that a successful deal would invigorate U.S. security partnerships in the region, and that an agreement should be considered solely for its economic impact. They maintain that past trade pacts have had a limited impact on broad foreign policy dynamics and that U.S. bilateral relations are based on each country's broader national interests.

The Administration is also pursuing strategic economic goals in the TPP. Through the agreement, proponents argue, the United States can play a leading role in "writing the rules" for commerce with key trading partners, addressing gaps in current multilateral trade rules, and setting a precedent for future regional and bilateral FTA negotiations or multilateral trade talks at the World Trade Organization (WTO). The core of this argument is the assertion that the TPP's potential components—including tariff and non-tariff liberalization, strong intellectual property rights and investment protections, and labor and environmental provisions—would build upon the U.S.-led economic system that has expanded world trade and investment enormously since the end of World War II.

Although most U.S. observers agree it is in the U.S. interest to lead in establishing global and regional trade rules, less consensus exists on what those rules should be, yielding some criticism on the strength and breadth of various TPP provisions. In addition, some argue that crafting new rules through "mega-regional" agreements rather than the WTO could undermine the multilateral trading system, create competing trading blocs, lead to trade diversion, and marginalize the countries not participating in regional initiatives.

China is not a TPP member, but features prominently in discussion of the agreement's potential strategic effects. Some argue that China is attempting to create a regional order that seeks to minimize U.S. presence and power. In this line of reasoning, the TPP serves as a counter to growing Chinese economic and political influence, implying that failure to conclude TPP could, in effect, allow China to shape regional rules of commerce and diplomacy through its own trade and investment initiatives. Others, however, argue that TPP is complementary to other FTAs and trade agreements throughout the region, including those championed by China, and that new members—possibly including China—will be critical for the TPP to influence regional norms.

Trade agreements occur at the intersection of foreign and domestic policy, which can create tensions in balancing competing policy priorities. Key issues Congress faces as it continues its role regarding TPP include (1) how strongly to weigh geo-political implications of TPP; (2) the potential impact of the TPP on the multilateral trading system and other trade and economic institutions; and (3) the possible expansion of the agreement to include additional members.

OVERVIEW

The Obama Administration has pursued the proposed 12-nation Trans-Pacific Partnership (TPP) free trade agreement (FTA) negotiations as the primary economic component of its "strategic rebalance" of U.S. foreign policy priorities to the Asia-Pacific region.[1] The 12 participating countries announced the conclusion of negotiations and released the text of the agreement in late 2015, and signed the proposed FTA on February 4, 2016.[2] The TPP aims to liberalize and establish rules and disciplines governing trade and investment among its 12 members,[3] and has broad implications for U.S. relations in the region.

Congress had an active role in the TPP negotiations through oversight, consultations with the Administration, and formal negotiating objectives established in Trade Promotion Authority (TPA) legislation. Ultimately, Congress would need to pass implementing legislation before the TPP could take effect in the United States. The potential impacts of the agreement may be an active area of debate during the second session of the 114th Congress.

According to TPP proponents, including U.S. Trade Representative Michael Froman, "the TPP's significance is not just economic, it's strategic."[4] The term strategic has been used in the context of the TPP debate to capture a range of arguments encompassing both geo-political and geoeconomic aspects of U.S. policy, making it difficult to define precisely. In broad terms, however, arguments about the TPP's strategic importance relate to the United States using the agreement as a tool to exert influence in the region and beyond, in both economic and broader political and security spheres, and creating conditions that facilitate other U.S. policy tools. Such arguments maintain that through the TPP, the United States can

- strengthen regional alliances and partnerships;
- maintain U.S. leadership and influence in the Asia-Pacific region;
- enhance U.S. national security;
- liberalize trade, encourage market-oriented reforms, and drive economic growth;
- strengthen regional and potentially global trade architecture; and
- establish and update regional trade rules and disciplines consistent with U.S. interests and modern commercial realities.

China is not a TPP member, but features prominently in analysis of U.S. influence in the region. Beijing's economic rise and active trade and investment initiatives in the region form an important backdrop to the strategic aspects of the TPP negotiations. Now the world's second largest economy, China has grown much faster than the United States over the past decade as a trade partner for most Asian countries. Over the past several years, Beijing has initiated or supported a broad set of trade and investment initiatives to spur development in the region. Some analysts argue that through these initiatives China is attempting to create a regional order that seeks to minimize U.S. presence and power. (See "China's Regional "Vision" section below.)

As a result, those championing the agreement, including the President, often cast TPP as a vehicle for maintaining U.S. leadership in Asia and establishing trade and investment rules and norms with an eye towards China.[5] Others contend that casting the TPP as an effort to "counter" Chinese initiatives is unproductive, and could create negative perceptions of U.S. intentions, both in China and elsewhere in the region. Some also argue that in many ways U.S. and Chinese goals for trade liberalization and rules and norms in the region may be mutually reinforcing rather than competing.

Trade agreements inevitably exist at the intersection of domestic and foreign policy and include both economic and political elements. This can create a tension in balancing various policy priorities, particularly for those policymakers who may support the TPP on some grounds but not others. Some opponents of the agreement argue that focusing on the strategic elements of the TPP distracts the debate from what they view should be its main criteria: the agreement's potential impact on the U.S. economy. While both TPP critics and supporters cite different estimates of economic outcomes to support their positions, the broader strategic implications tend to be highlighted by proponents, and can be difficult to quantify despite their potential significance.

This report will examine selected strategic arguments presented by the Administration, as well as by TPP proponents and opponents. Other CRS reports[6] address the specific trade negotiations and economic effects. This report focuses generally on the Asia-Pacific region, with particular emphasis on implications for Asia.[7] The report also raises strategic issues Congress may consider as it examines a final TPP agreement and potentially debates future legislation to approve and implement it.

GEO-POLITICAL ARGUMENTS SURROUNDING TPP

Since the end of World War II, the United States has advanced trade agreements and institutions such as FTAs to promote its broader foreign policy goals. The United States signed its first FTA with Israel in 1985, and many observers argue that political solidarity with Israel weighed more heavily than its economic value at the time.[8] In the 2000s, many observers saw U.S. FTAs with Bahrain, Morocco, and Oman as based not just on economic, but also on security and foreign policy objectives—primarily helping forge closer cooperation on efforts to combat terrorism. The first U.S. FTA in Asia entered into force in 2004 with Singapore, a close U.S. security partner with enormous strategic interests in liberalizing trade.

Obama Administration officials and many of the TPP's proponents argue that U.S. trade policy initiatives in Asia, particularly the TPP, have considerable geostrategic importance. The Administration's 2015 National Security Strategy stated:

> Sustaining our leadership depends on shaping an emerging global economic order that continues to reflect our interests and values. Despite its success, our rules-based system is now competing against alternative, less-open models.... To meet this challenge, we must be strategic in the use of our economic strength to set new rules of the road, strengthen our partnerships, and promote inclusive development.[9]

To some observers, TPP is an important test of U.S. credibility as a regional leader. The proposed agreement is the Obama Administration's signature economic initiative in the Asia-Pacific region. Some observers have argued that if the agreement is not approved by Congress, the entire rebalancing strategy could be seen as relatively weak and the United States will be seen as divided on how important it considers its leadership role in Asia.[10] Administration officials argue that the agreement is a key signal that the United States is actively integrated into Asia's economic and diplomatic structures. In a 2014 article in *Foreign Affairs*, U.S. Trade Representative Froman argued, "For many of the countries that would be party to the TPP, the economic benefits of the agreement are further sweetened by expectations that the United States will become more deeply embedded in the region."[11]

These arguments are echoed by many in the Asia-Pacific region, particularly among TPP negotiating partners. At a regional security conference in Singapore in May 2015, Singapore Prime Minister Lee Hsien Loong said, "... whatever the merits or demerits of individual line items of trade covered in the TPP, the agreement has a wider strategic significance. Getting the TPP done will deepen links on both sides of the Pacific. Failing to get the TPP done will hurt the credibility and standing of the U.S. not just in Asia, but worldwide."[12]

Some proponents also argue that concluding the TPP would be an important aspect of a broader U.S. strategy to develop and strengthen regional institutions in ways that foster cooperation and the peaceful resolution of differences through respect for rules and norms. In 2013, then National Security Advisor Tom Donilon wrote: "Just as our security alliances across two oceans have brought stability that extends far beyond our treaty partners, U.S. economic diplomacy today can advance global prosperity by strengthening the international rules and norms that make trade and growth possible."[13]

Linkages between the TPP and the promotion of broader diplomatic and security interests have become a strong part of the Administration's arguments for TPP. In an April 2015 speech providing a status report on the "rebalancing," Secretary of Defense Ashton Carter stated that "passing TPP is as important to me as another aircraft carrier."[14] Other TPP proponents have said that the agreement will reinforce U.S. alliances and partnerships in East Asia.[15] However, when elaborating on security rationales for supporting passage of TPP, many of the agreement's backers do not identify specific, concrete ways that a successful deal would invigorate U.S. security partnerships in the region.

Some critics of TPP assert that the strength or weakness of broader bilateral political and security relationships depend more upon countries' assessment of their security interests than on whether they have a trade agreement with the United States.[16] For instance, they contend, it arguably is difficult to pinpoint how, if at all, the South Korea-United States Free Trade Agreement (KORUS FTA), which went into effect in 2012, by itself has altered either South Korea's or the United States' fundamental interests on the Korean Peninsula or in Northeast Asia. Put another way, the short-term strength of the U.S.-South Korea alliance likely is determined by factors such as the two countries' perception of threats from China or North Korea, rather than by the presence of the KORUS FTA. Likewise, few observers believe the future of the U.S.-Japan alliance depends heavily on the TPP's success or failure. In recent years, Japan's own strategic and political calculations appear to have been the primary drivers behind its moves to deepen strategic cooperation with the United States.

TPP may have a larger impact on countries with which the U.S. relationship is not as close. In Vietnam's case, for instance, some argue that a successful outcome in the TPP negotiations would support reform-oriented decisionmakers by requiring the government to enact deeper market-oriented institutional changes that may be required to implement their commitments under TPP provisions. In some cases, these same individuals may also support deepening relations with the United States.[17] Many Vietnamese leaders would see TPP approval as a sign that the United States welcomes closer ties and more normal relations with the country. Failure to approve the agreement, some argue, could negatively affect Vietnam's perception of the United States as a reliable partner, at least in the economic realm.

Some TPP proponents contend that the agreement will help the United States, as Defense Secretary Carter has said, "promote a global order that reflects both our interests and our values."[18] Historically, U.S. interests have included the establishment of a rules-based trading system founded on principles of transparency, openness, and non-discrimination, but less clear, and less often specified by proponents is the link between the TPP's trade rules and the security realm.

One indirect way that economically large trade agreements such as TPP may affect U.S. security relationships is by altering countries' *perception* of where their strategic interests lie. Each major agreement, the argument runs, signals that the participating countries are key partners, and merit treatment as such. By this line of reasoning, approving and implementing TPP would help to "lock-in" the United States' Pacific presence, keeping the United States closely connected to developments in the Pacific as countries in the region become wealthier and more powerful.[19] Similarly, implementing the TPP could send the message to other countries that the Pacific Rim is a priority of U.S. policymakers.

The flip side of this argument is that many Asian policymakers—correctly or not—could interpret a failure of TPP in the United States as a symbol of the United States' declining interest in the region and inability to assert leadership. A former U.S. ambassador to China was quoted in June 2015 saying: "Domestically we tend to view trade through a political prism by way of winners and losers ... In Asia, it's seen as directly tied to our leadership and commitment to the region. A failed TPP would create an influence vacuum that others, primarily China, would fill."[20]

Many argue that U.S. credibility in Asia currently is in question, during a time when China's rise and North Korea's growing nuclear and missile capabilities are testing the U.S.-based rules system and challenging U.S. influence.[21] Some TPP backers take this a step further, arguing that relationships such as that between the United States and Japan "would suffer from a period of mutual recriminations and loss of trust and cooperation."[22] In a scenario where a TPP agreement is rejected by Congress, thus negating any politically challenging concessions that others made through negotiation, the loss of trust and cooperation could be particularly pronounced.

THE TPP AND U.S. TRADE POLICY

The TPP may also have implications for U.S. influence on regional and global efforts to shape trade and investment. Proponents argue that the rules established in the TPP will promote economic growth and advance U.S. interests by influencing trade regimes at several levels:

- encouraging market opening and economic reforms among TPP's current members, particularly in emerging markets such as Malaysia and Vietnam;
- creating incentives for other Asia-Pacific nations to follow suit, to match the preferential access that TPP member countries would gain in major markets such as the United States and Japan; and
- addressing new trade barriers through new trade rules and disciplines, laying groundwork to influence and potentially spur future multilateral or plurilateral negotiations at the WTO or future FTA negotiations, and update critical gaps in existing trade rules.

U.S. Trade Policy in Context

Central to U.S. negotiating objectives in the TPP is the goal to update the rules-based trading system.[23] Since World War II, the United States, primarily through multilateral fora, has sought to expand economic engagement through trade as a mechanism for generating broader economic growth and prosperity. Through "rounds" of trade liberalization negotiations under the General Agreement on Tariffs and Trade (GATT), the United States led in liberalizing tariff and non-tariff barriers, setting rules and norms based on transparency, non-discrimination, and most-favored nation treatment. This led eventually to the establishment of the international rules-based trade architecture of the World Trade Organization (WTO), the successor to the GATT.

Launched in 2001, the current WTO multilateral trade negotiations—the WTO Doha Development Agenda (Doha Round)—has largely stalled due to persistent differences among its members.24 In the meantime, global commerce has adapted to rapid advances in technology, such that current multilateral trade rules do not address some critical aspects of today's trading environment, including issues related to digital trade and the role of state-owned enterprises. This has led some countries, including the United States, to pursue new or advanced trade rules and further liberalization through bilateral and regional agreements, such as the TPP.

Strategic Aspects of U.S. Trade Policy

TPP proponents argue that the agreement's scale gives it considerable strategic heft, by creating an economically significant bloc of nations that has agreed to its broad disciplines. The 11 other TPP countries account for 37% of U.S. trade, and together the 12 economies account for 37% of global GDP.[25] The TPP's economic significance could grow, as the TPP members have negotiated an agreement open to new countries willing to adhere to its provisions and make satisfactory market access commitments.

In some emerging economies, the TPP could give domestic reformers the political cover necessary to push forward with their own reform agendas, citing such reforms as necessary to gain greater access to the U.S. market. Arguably, these incentives could also help promote U.S. goals such as respect for internationally recognized worker rights and practices aimed at protecting the environment, such as curbing trade in endangered species.

Beyond these effects, proponents argue that an implemented TPP will draw interest from other countries, as those not party to the agreement may begin to face competitive disadvantages. Such competitive pressure, they argue, could expand the reach of the TPP's rules, driving further trade and investment liberalization in the region. One could look to Japan's involvement in the TPP negotiations—reportedly in part a response to the completion of the U.S. FTA with South Korea—as evidence of such a dynamic.[26]

Others, however, note that the TPP as presently constituted does not include some of Asia's largest economies, including China, India, and Indonesia, so even if it is ratified and implemented, they say it will not create a comprehensive set of "rules of the road" for trade and investment in the Asia-Pacific.[27]

Some experts argue that the influence of TPP's trade rules may depend on whether new members seek to join it in the future. Several large Asian countries, including Indonesia, the Philippines, South Korea, and Thailand, have publicly expressed interest in joining a "second round" of TPP members once the agreement is implemented, giving weight to the Administration's argument that the domain of TPP's influence may grow. Taiwan has also expressed interest in membership. Many Asian nations, however, face considerable current domestic opposition to joining TPP, as do some of the current TPP parties now debating ratification.[28] Many analysts argue that U.S. FTA partners in Asia and Latin America, particularly South Korea and Colombia, may be among the most likely countries to seek entry in the TPP in the near future.[29]

Beyond regional implications, TPP proponents also argue that the size and economic significance of "mega-regionals," such as the TPP and the U.S.-EU Trans-Atlantic Trade and Investment Partnership (T-TIP), may help spur long-stalled negotiations at the multilateral level and influence their direction.[30] They argue that the rules established in the TPP that go beyond existing WTO commitments and address new trade barriers could become the basis for future negotiations at the WTO, including on a plurilateral basis.

Critics argue, however, that these bilateral and regional trade negotiations may draw resources and attention from and thereby impede multilateral initiatives. If the locus of trade negotiations shifts away from the WTO and the rules of the body no longer reflect global standards of trade policy, it could undermine the legitimacy of the organization in other aspects of its work, such as dispute settlement. The WTO's role as a force for future trade liberalization could be dampened. Mega-regionals could also add to the complexity of the trading system by creating overlapping and differing rules and commitments, instead of operating through multilateral rules established at the WTO that are applicable to nearly all world trading partners.[30]

TPP and Other Asian Regional Trade Initiatives

TPP negotiations are one of a number of ongoing trade negotiations in the Asia-Pacific region, many of which do not include the United States and may differ in their structure and aims. Perhaps the most significant negotiation outside the TPP, particularly in terms of its membership, is the Regional Comprehensive Economic Partnership (RCEP), which would join the 10 ASEAN members and six nations with which ASEAN has trade agreements—Australia, China, India, Japan, New Zealand, and South Korea—in one collective FTA.[31] The United States does not have an FTA with ASEAN and has not expressed an interest in joining the RCEP negotiations.

Though RCEP's final provisions have yet to be determined, a comparison of the ASEAN trade agreements on which it is being built and the components of the finalized TPP provides some indication of potential differences.[32] A 2013 examination of ASEAN trade agreements shows that they have been less comprehensive in terms of trade liberalization than the proposed TPP.[33] In addition, the existing ASEAN FTAs often do not include or have less extensive intellectual property rights, investment, and labor and environmental provisions than the TPP.[34] The TPP also includes disciplines on state-owned enterprises (SOEs), a topic unlikely to be addressed in RCEP.

Due in part to these potential differences, some argue that RCEP presents an alternative, and possibly a challenge, to U.S. efforts to craft trade rules through the TPP.[35] Others believe the proposed agreements can be complementary and both will lead to economic growth benefitting the region as a whole.[36] Notably, seven countries are in both RCEP and the TPP, and presumably have an interest in ensuring some degree of compatibility and synergy between the two agreements (*Figure 1*).

At this point, it is unclear how these two regional undertakings may affect one another and how they would affect the existing trade architecture in the region. This will depend in part on their timing. With negotiations concluded, the TPP is at a more advanced stage than RCEP, whose members agreed in November 2015 that negotiations would continue into 2016. A delay in the ratification and implementation process for TPP, however, could alter that sequencing.

All 12 TPP countries, and 11 RCEP countries are also members of the 21-member Asia-Pacific Economic Cooperation (APEC) forum, a body for dialogue on and establishing nonbinding commitments toward the goals of open and free trade and investment within the region. APEC members have discussed the possible creation of a broad Free Trade Area of the Asia-Pacific (FTAAP) since 2006—a goal that both China and the United States have supported. In the statement issued at APEC's annual Leaders Meeting in 2014, the group's leaders recognized both TPP and RCEP as "possible pathways" to the FTAAP.[37]

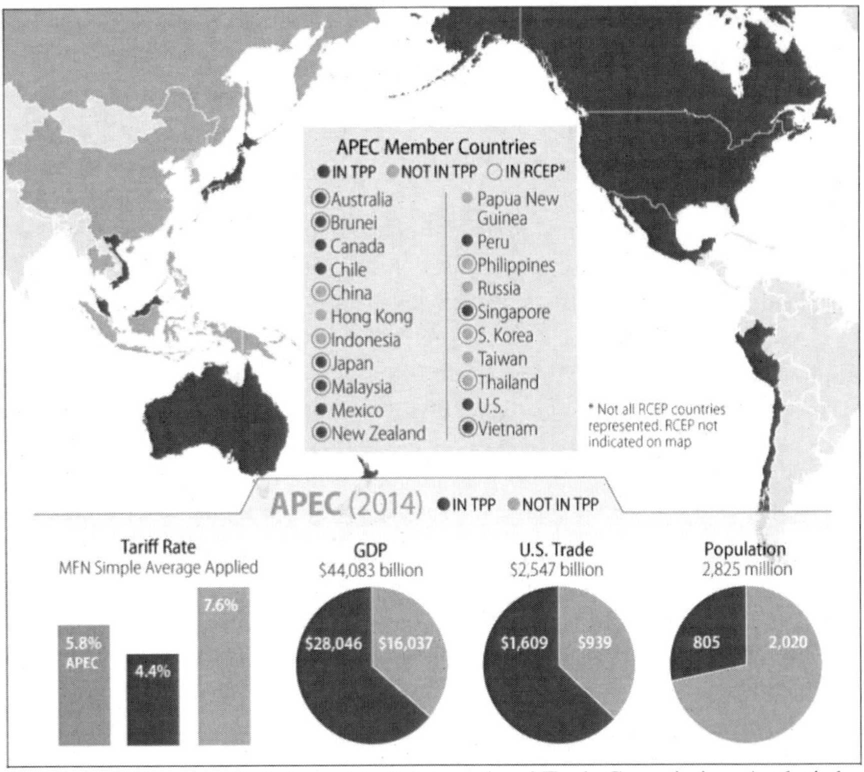

Source: Data from WTO, IMF, and U.S. International Trade Commission. Analysis by CRS.

Notes: APEC does not include all major Asia-Pacific economies, notably omitting India, which is currently seeking to join the group. RCEP countries not in APEC are Burma, Cambodia, Laos, and India.

Figure 1. APEC and TPP Membership.

CHINA AND U.S. POLICY IN ASIA

China has figured prominently in debates about the TPP and broader U.S. policy in Asia. As the world's second largest economy (on a nominal dollar basis) and largest trading economy, China's inclusion in, or exclusion from, the TPP in the future may have important implications for the United States, as well as the Asia-Pacific region. President Obama and other TPP proponents also argue that China's growing international influence increases the strategic importance of completing the proposed TPP. Some analysts go further, arguing that China is attempting to create a regional order that seeks to minimize U.S. presence and power and that TPP is a necessary means of countering this effort.[38]

Many analysts argue that decades of expanding Chinese trade and investment, as well as new Chinese trade and investment initiatives around the region, have created a vision of regional economic development that is different from that advocated by the United States, and potentially not in the U.S. interest. The proposed TPP, its proponents argue, would allow the United States to help shape a model in line with U.S. interests by creating rules and norms that other regional nations may ultimately opt to join. Due to the TPP's size and economic importance, the argument runs, it would help to influence China's economic—and potentially diplomatic—decisions in ways that are more favorable to U.S. economic, diplomatic, and security interests. As President Obama stated in a June 2015 interview:

> the fact is that if we have 11 of the leading economies in the Asia-Pacific region, who have agreed to enforceable labor standards, enforceable environmental standards, strong IP protections, non-discrimination against foreign firms that are operating, access to those markets, reduce tariffs, then China is going to have to at least take those international norms into account.[39]

A completed TPP could also encourage China to further liberalize its economic and trade regime in order to eventually join the agreement. It might also give some reformers in China a measure of political cover to press for deeper reform, beyond Beijing's WTO commitments.

To others, such arguments unnecessarily cast Asia's largest economy as an outlier in regional economic development and may overstate the degree to which Chinese initiatives are likely to influence regional trade and investment rules.[40] Such arguments stress several points. First, they note that if China's leaders perceive that TPP is being used as a tool to constrain Chinese interests, they could respond in ways that are inimical to U.S. interests. Second, they stress that China is proceeding with economic initiatives that others in Asia may see as helpful to their own economic development, given the region's extensive needs for infrastructure and other investment; they argue, therefore, that if countries in the region see the United States as opposing these initiatives, the United States may risk being seen as obstructionist, which could lead some in Asia to question U.S. commitments to regional development. Third, they stress that other Asian nations have their own trade policies and are unlikely to adopt policies they see as not in their interest—whether they are part of "models" that are American, Chinese or otherwise.

China's Regional "Vision"

China's leaders are striving to continue the transformation of their nation into a prosperous and respected major power, and the fulfillment of these goals they see as predicated on three conditions: 1) a strong economy; 2) a strong defense; and 3) a respected role on the global stage. The Chinese government is currently pursuing a number of policies designed to strengthen its economy and increase China's role in the overall global economic system. China's plans to construct a land-based Silk Road Economic Belt and the Maritime Silk Road (jointly known as the "One Belt, One Road") to create new linkages to Europe, the Middle East, central Asia, and Southeast Asia. In doing so, they seek to facilitate trade and foster greater economic development and integration.[41] New financial institutions—such as the newly-created Asian Infrastructure Investment Bank (AIIB)[42] and the Silk Road Fund—are aimed at providing the capital to finance the "One Belt, One Road" initiative and other major economic development projects. China's efforts to gradually increase the overseas use of its currency, the renminbi, are intended to simplify the transactions Chinese financial institutions use to support Chinese assistance programs, reduce the commercial risk for Chinese companies engaged in international trade and investment, and enhance China's global economic stature. Finally, Chinese leaders see the establishment of RCEP as laying the foundations for a broader FTAAP, which could be seen as a set of regional rules and norms inspired, at least in part, by Chinese leadership.

China's leaders also seek to reform existing multilateral institutions to reflect what they see as the geopolitical situation of today, rather than that of the post-World War II era. China is taking an active role in promoting reforms of the United Nations, the International Monetary Fund, and the World Bank. The establishment of the AIIB in part is an attempt to offer an alternative model for the various multilateral development banks, such as the Asian Development Bank (ADB), to adopt. However, it is unclear at this early stage of its development whether the AIIB will be more distinct from or more in line with these international institutions.

China's efforts to reshape or create new economic institutions are matched by its actions in the diplomatic and security spheres, where Beijing appears to be attempting to reduce or counter U.S. influence. For instance, according to many analysts, China has attempted to refashion the Conference on Interaction and Confidence Building Measures in Asia (CICA), a 26-member group that spans the Eurasian continent and does not include the United States, into a new Asian continental security system to counter the U.S. alliance network.[43] China also has undertaken extensive reclamation and construction on several disputed reefs in the South China Sea,[44] moves that many see as laying the groundwork for countering U.S. naval power in the Western Pacific.

China and the TPP

China's publicly-stated views of the TPP have varied and appear to have changed over time, especially as more countries have joined the TPP negotiations. After the United States joined the TPP talks in 2008, China's media portrayed the TPP as a U.S.-dominated process that was largely aimed at advancing U.S. economic interests over the rest of Asia and isolating China by excluding it from the talks. U.S. officials have countered such portrayals. In December 2014, for instance, President Obama said: "... there's been some suggestion that by doing TPP we're trying to contain or disadvantage China. We're actually not.... [W]e hope that ... China actually joins us in not necessarily formally being a member of TPP but in adopting some of the best practices that ensure fairness in operations."[45]

China's publicly-stated criticisms of the U.S. role in the TPP process appear to have softened somewhat shortly after Japan joined the TPP talks in April 2013.[46] In October 2014, China's Vice Finance Minister Zhu Guangyao stated that a TPP agreement was "incomplete without China." In November 2014, Chinese Premier Li Keqiang in a speech before the East Asia Summit, stated: "China is open to negotiations on the TPP. In our view, various FTA arrangements can play a positive role in fostering a just and free international and regional trade order."[47]

U.S. officials have said China is welcome to join the TPP, although Chinese officials often state that many of the standards and provisions of the proposed agreement would be difficult for China to implement.[48] President Obama said in June 2015 that China had "already started putting out feelers about the possibilities of them participating at some point" in the TPP.[49]

Several analysts contend that the ultimate aim of the United States is to integrate China more fully into deeper and greater commitments to further liberalize trade and establish new trade rules and disciplines addressing issues not currently, or inadequately, addressed in the WTO multilateral trading system. For example, one former Obama Administration official argues that "an agreement with high standards like the TPP could subject China to new, higher-standard rules, and discourage China from trying to weaken or soften the existing trade rules through other channels."[50] In addition, the United States is currently negotiating a bilateral investment treaty (BIT) with China that could boost bilateral investment flows and facilitate its future potential participation in TPP.[51]

Issues for Congress

Since the United States joined the TPP in 2008, Congress has played a direct role in guiding and overseeing the negotiations. Congress approved legislation to renew U.S. Trade Promotion Authority (TPA) in 2015 to establish U.S. trade negotiating objectives and provide for the expedited consideration of legislation to implement U.S. trade agreements concluded by the President, among other provisions. Congress will have a direct role in considering TPP and implementing legislation.

As Congress considers the TPP agreement and its strategic elements, it might consider examining a number of issues, including the following:

- *Whether TPP Furthers a Broader Foreign Policy Strategy.* TPP proponents argue that the proposed agreement is part of a broad foreign policy strategy to promote greater respect for international rules and norms in the Asia-Pacific region. If it is approved, they argue, the implications could further other U.S. diplomatic and security goals, beyond the trade realm. By encouraging a diverse group of nations to accept the rules and disciplines contained in the TPP, the argument holds, the United States will have reinforced U.S. leadership in the region, given space to Asia-Pacific leaders who seek greater economic and (perhaps) political reform, and encouraged a group of nations to adopt a more U.S.-supportive foreign policy outlook. Congress may wish to consider how deeply it accepts these arguments, and whether it sees the proposed agreement as part of a well-considered and broader foreign policy strategy.

- *How Deeply to Weigh These Strategic Arguments.* In considering an agreement as broad as the TPP, Congress may weigh trade-offs among the agreement's many potential implications. Are the TPP's strategic implications a critical consideration for Congress, or do they distract the debate from the TPP's more direct impact on the U.S. economy? How do these different arguments relate? Are the potential strategic benefits of the agreement contingent on its ability to drive economic growth and prosperity? For those who support the TPP on some grounds but not others, what rank should be given to various aspects of the agreement? Does the argument that the TPP is an important measure of U.S. leadership in Asia outweigh potential concerns arising from individual terms of the agreement?
- *Membership Expansion.* Some argue that the TPP's ultimate strategic impact will depend on whether a broader group of nations ultimately decides to join it. To other observers, the proposed TPP, established by like-minded countries, represents the best opportunity for the United States to pursue regional and broader multilateral trade policy goals currently unattainable in the WTO and other fora. Has the agreement struck the right balance between trade liberalization and establishing rules that are most beneficial for U.S. economic interests, while at the same time remaining attractive to a broader set of regional actors that could enhance the agreement's strategic value?
- *Implications of Failed Ratification*. From the standpoint of promoting greater U.S. leadership and influence in the region, Congress may wish to consider whether delays or failure to ratify and implement the agreement would set back these goals. The TPP took more than five years to conclude, and if rejected by Congress, it could take several years for an alternative, U.S.-led agreement, if any, to take shape. Meanwhile, other countries in the region continue to pursue their own trade arrangements. Would a failure to ratify the TPP impact foreign governments' views on U.S. leadership and credibility in the region, or do other foreign policies, including U.S. military presence, ultimately shape such views?

- *Implications for Countries Outside the TPP.* The TPP's 12 participating countries do not include several in the Asia-Pacific region that are strategically and economically important. Some observers urge the United States to enunciate strategies that reinforce U.S. economic engagement more broadly across the region, beyond the current TPP membership, in part so that countries that currently are not in the TPP do not conclude that Washington is neglecting or ignoring them. Congress may wish to consider whether existing U.S. economic initiatives in Asia are sufficient to achieve broad goals of furthering U.S. influence across the region, or whether other economic initiatives are advisable as an assurance of U.S. commitment to the region. If other initiatives are advisable, which nations or multilateral groups should be targeted? Congress also may wish to consider whether it is strategically important that TPP expand to include other countries outside the region.
- *Implications for the Multilateral Trading System.* Analysts hold mixed views as to how "mega-regional" negotiations may impact the multilateral trading system as represented by the WTO. While some see such agreements as an opportunity for the United States to advance new trade rules and disciplines that may eventually be incorporated in multilateral initiatives, others worry they may usurp legitimacy from the WTO and may negatively impact countries not involved in their negotiation. From a strategic standpoint, Congress may wish to consider whether the proposed TPP will further eventual WTO multilateral trade liberalization or lead to greater fragmentation of the global trading system. Congress also may wish to consider whether to seek new trade initiatives at the global level, either to assure that the TPP has the effect of spurring momentum at the global level or to address potential concerns that the TPP shifts the center of trade discussions away from the WTO.

End Notes

[1] U.S. involvement in the TPP negotiations began in 2008 under the Bush Administration as the United States decided to participate in expanding the existing P-4 agreement among Brunei, Chile, New Zealand, and Singapore. For more information on the background of the TPP, see CRS Report R44278, The Trans-Pacific Partnership (TPP): In Brief, by Ian F. Fergusson, Mark A. McMinimy, and Brock R. Williams and CRS In Focus IF10000, The Trans-Pacific Partnership (TPP): An Overview, by Brock R. Williams and Ian F. Fergusson.

[2] USTR, "Trans-Pacific Partnership Ministers' Statement," February 4, 2016, http://www.tpp.mfat.govt.nz/assets/docs/Trans-Pacific%20Partnership%20Ministers%20Statement%204%20Feb%202016.pdf. The full TPP text is at https://ustr.gov/trade-agreements/free-trade-agreements/trans-pacific-partnership/tpp-full-text.

[3] The countries participating in the TPP negotiations with the United States are Australia, Brunei, Canada, Chile, Japan, Malaysia, Mexico, New Zealand, Peru, Singapore, and Vietnam.

[4] USTR, "Remarks by Ambassador Michael Froman at the CSIS Asian Architecture Conference," September 22, 2015.

[5] White House, "Statement by the President on the Trans-Pacific Partnership," press release, October 5, 2015, https://www.whitehouse.gov/the-press-office/2015/10/05/statement-president-trans-pacific-partnership.

[6] For more information on the TPP negotiations, see CRS Report R42694, The Trans-Pacific Partnership (TPP) Negotiations and Issues for Congress, coordinated by Ian F. Fergusson, CRS Report R42344, Trans-Pacific Partnership (TPP) Countries: Comparative Trade and Economic Analysis, by Brock R. Williams, and CRS In Focus IF10000, The Trans-Pacific Partnership (TPP): An Overview, by Brock R. Williams and Ian F. Fergusson.

[7] In addition to countries in Asia, the TPP includes five countries in the Western Hemisphere: Canada, Chile, Mexico, Peru, and the United States.

[8] At the time, few bilateral or regional FTAs were being pursued by the United States or other countries. Instead, trade negotiations focused on multilateral efforts in the General Agreement on Tariffs and Trade (GATT), the predecessor to the World Trade Organization (WTO).

[9] White House, "National Security Strategy," February 2015. https://www.whitehouse.gov/sites/default/files/docs/2015_national_security_strategy.pdf.

[10] Jeffrey A. Bader and David Dollar, "Why the TPP Is the Linchpin of the Asia Rebalance," Brookings.edu, July 28, 2015.

[11] Michael Froman, "The Strategic Argument of Trade," Foreign Affairs, November/December 2014.

[12] Prime Minister's Office of Singapore, "Transcript of Keynote Speech by Prime Minister Lee Hsien Loong at the Shangri-La Dialogue 29 May 2015." http://www.pmo.gov.sg/media centre/transcript-keynote-speech-prime-ministerlee-hsien-loong-shangri-la-dialogue-29-may-2015.

[13] Tom Donilon, "The President's Free Trade Path to Prosperity," Wall Street Journal, April 15, 2013.

[14] U.S. Department of Defense, "Asia-Pacific Remarks," Secretary of Defense Ashton Carter, McCain Institute, Arizona State University, April 6, 2015.

[15] Dennis C. Blair, "Who Decides Pacific Trade?" New York Times, November 5, 2014.

[16] Daniel Slane and Michael Wessel, "The TPP: Why It Won't Address Security Concerns with China," Renewing America blog, Council on Foreign Relations, May 15, 2015.

[17] Truong-Minh Vu & Nguyen Nhat-Anh, "Vietnam Debates the TPP," CSIS cogitAsia blog, September 24, 2014.

[18] Carter, "Asia-Pacific Remarks," April 6, 2015.

[19] Daniel Drezner, "The Trans-Pacific Partnership is About More than Trade," Washington Post, May 7, 2015.

[20] Jon Huntsman, quoted in Peter Baker, "The Trans-Pacific Partnership and a President's Legacy," New York Times. June 14, 2015.

[21] Ellen L. Frost, "In Asia, U.S. Economic Leadership Is Under Attack," The National Interest, January 8, 2015.

[22] Dennis C. Blair, "Who Decides Pacific Trade?" New York Times, November 5, 2014.

[23] Michael Froman, interview by Gerald F. Seib, "The U.S. Trade Agenda and the Trans-Pacific Partnership," Council on Foreign Relations, October 15, 2015.

[24] Despite the stalled Doha Round, some progress in negotiations at the WTO has been made, including the Trade Facilitation Agreement, now undergoing ratification procedures by member countries. For more information, see CRS In Focus IF10002, The World Trade Organization, by Ian F. Fergusson and Rachel F. Fefer.

[25] CRS Report R42344, Trans-Pacific Partnership (TPP) Countries: Comparative Trade and Economic Analysis, by Brock R. Williams.

[26] Japan, whose firms compete with South Korea's in several sectors, declared its interest in the TPP negotiations one month after the implementing legislation for KORUS was signed by President Obama in October 2011.

[27] South Korea is also not currently participating in the TPP, but given its FTA with the United States, it adheres to rules of a similar nature to TPP, at least in its trade with the United States.

[28] See, for instance, "Aquino government won't seek to join, trade chief says," Nikkei Weekly, March 31, 2015; "Treaty holds no attraction," Bangkok Post, October 22, 2014. "Indonesia and the Trans-Pacific Partnership: To Join or Not?" The Jakarta Globe, January 22, 2014.

[29] "Pacific Alliance Seeks Leverage by Joining Bigger Groupings," Financial Times, September 27, 2015. Colombia and the three Latin American countries currently participating in the TPP negotiations (Chile, Mexico, and Peru) are the founding members of the Pacific Alliance, a Latin American trade bloc of countries embracing economic openness and each with extensive existing trade agreement networks. For more information, see CRS Report R43748, The Pacific Alliance: A Trade Integration Initiative in Latin America, by M. Angeles Villarreal.

[30] Some argue the conclusion of the North American Free Trade Agreement (NAFTA), among the United States, Canada, and Mexico, played such a role in advancing the multilateral Uruguay Round negotiations in the 1990s. The Uruguay Round agreement was signed in April 1994, nearly seven years after it was launched but less than a year after legislation implementing NAFTA was signed by the U.S. Congress.

[31] The 10 ASEAN members are Brunei, Burma (Myanmar), Cambodia, Indonesia, Laos, Malaysia, the Philippines, Singapore, Thailand, and Vietnam.

[32] The countries involved in RCEP have ambitions for more comprehensive liberalization than they have achieved in the existing ASEAN FTAs. For more information on RCEP, see CRS In Focus IF10342, What Is the Regional Comprehensive Economic Partnership?, by Michael F. Martin et al.

[33] According to analysis by the Economic Research Institute for ASEAN and East Asia (ERIA) of the ASEAN FTAs with the six countries participating in the RCEP negotiations (Australia, China, Japan, India, New Zealand, and South Korea), the percentage of tariff lines with eventual duty elimination under the respective FTAs range from 79.6% for the ASEAN-India FTA to 95.7% for the ASEAN-Australia-New Zealand FTA. By contrast, according to analysis by CRS, the TPP would eventually eliminate duties on more than 99% of tariff lines, on average, across the 12 countries. Yoshifumi Fukunaga and Ikumo Isono, Taking ASEAN+1 FTAs Towards the RCEP: A Mapping Study, Economic Research Institute for ASEAN and East Asia, ERIA-DP-2013-02, January 2013, p. 8.

[34] Texts of the ASEAN FTAs can be found at the WTO website, http://rtais.wto.org/.

[35] Jeff Okun-Kozlowicki and Gabe Horwitz, The TPP: Who Will Set the Trade Rules for Asia?, Third Way, March 10, 2014.

[36] Simon Lester, Chinese Free Trade is No Threat to American Free Trade, Cato Institute, April 22, 2015.

[37] Asia-Pacific Economic Cooperation, 2010 Leaders' Declaration, November 2010, http://www.apec.org/MeetingPapers/Leaders-Declarations/2010/2010_aelm.aspx; 2014 Leader's Declaration, November 2014, http://www.apec.org/ Meeting-Papers/Leaders-Declarations/2014/2014_aelm/2014_aelm_annexa.aspx.

[38] For instance, see Takashi Terada, "Japan and the TPP Conclusion: Regional Order, Negotiations, and Domestic Adjustment," The Asan Forum, October 23, 2015, http://www.theasanforum.org/japan-and-the-tpp-conclusion regional-order-negotiations-and-domestic-adjustment/#a5.

[39] National Public Radio, Obama Says China Could Join Already Huge Asia Trade Deal, June 3, 2015, http://www.npr.org/sections/itsallpolitics/2015/06/03/411778624/obama-says-china-could-join-already-huge-asiatrade-deal.

[40] Chas Freeman, "Arguments for TPP Don't Make Sense," Boston Globe. May 31, 2015; Simon Lester, "Chinese Free Trade is No Threat to American Free Trade," Cato Institute. April 22, 2015.

[41] See CRS In Focus IF10273, China's "One Belt, One Road", by Susan V. Lawrence and Gabriel M. Nelson.

[42] See CRS In Focus IF10154, Asian Infrastructure Investment Bank, by Martin A. Weiss.

[43] Mike Green, "China Is Overreaching—Does the U.S. Have a Plan?" Foreign Policy.com, June 9, 2014, http://foreignpolicy.com/2014/06/09/china-is-overreaching-does-the-u-s-have-a-plan/.

[44] See CRS Report R44072, Chinese Land Reclamation in the South China Sea: Implications and Policy Options, by Ben Dolven et al.

[45] White House, "Remarks by the President at Meeting of the Export Council," December 11, 2014.

[46] The inclusion of Japan into the TPP talks was significant because of the size of its economy. With Japan, the combined economies of the 12 TPP members accounted for 37% of global GDP. This meant a TPP that did not include China could significantly affect the Chinese economy. For example, an October 2014 study by the Peterson Institute for International Economics estimated that China could lose as much as $100 billion of annual income and exports if a TPP agreement did not include China.

[47] ASEAN China Center, Remarks by H.E. Li Keqiang Premier of the State Council of the People's Republic of China at the Ninth East Asia Summit, November 14, 2014, available at http://www.asean-china-center.org/english/2014-11/14/c_133912792.htm.

[48] Foreign Policy, What Will the TPP Mean for China, October 7, 2015, http://foreign policy.com/2015/10/07/china-tpptrans-pacific-partnership-obama-us-trade-xi/.

[49] National Public Radio, Obama Says China Could Join Already Huge Asia Trade Deal, June 3, 2015, http://www.npr.org/sections/itsallpolitics/2015/06/03/411778624/obama-says-china-could-join-already-huge-asiatrade-deal.

[50] CSIS, the Trans-Pacific Partnership and China's Corresponding Strategies, June 2012, p. 4, http://csis.org/files/ publication/120620_Freeman_Brief.pdf.

[51] The BIT negotiations aim to establish mutual nondiscriminatory treatment of investments and reduce both market access barriers and ownership restrictions for U.S. firms in China, among other provisions. China has agreed to use the "negative list" approach in reducing ownership restrictions via the BIT, where all industries except those explicitly listed would be open to investments.

INDEX

2

A

B

C

D

E

F

G

H

I

J

K

L

O

P

Q

R

S

T

U

V

W